The Evolution of Southern Culture

The Evolution
of Southern Culture

EDITED BY
Numan V. Bartley

The University of Georgia Press
ATHENS AND LONDON

© 1988 by the University of Georgia Press
Athens, Georgia 30602
"The South and South Africa: Political
Foundations of White Supremacy" © 1988 by
George M. Fredrickson

Set in 10 on 12 Linotron 202 Sabon

The paper in this book meets the guidelines for
permanence and durability of the Committee on
Production Guidelines for Book Longevity of the
Council on Library Resources.

Printed in the United States of America

92 91 90 89 88   5 4 3 2 1

Library of Congress Cataloging in Publication Data

The Evolution of southern culture.

    Papers originally delivered at a symposium held at the
University of Georgia in October 1985.
    Includes bibliographies.
    1. Southern States—Civilization—Congresses.
I. Bartley, Numan V.
F209.E86   1988   975   87-19162
ISBN 0-8203-0993-1 (alk. paper)
ISBN 0-8203-1032-8 (pbk.: alk. paper)

British Library Cataloging in Publication Data available

Contents

Acknowledgments

This book developed from a symposium held at the University of Georgia in October 1985, part of the university's Bicentennial celebration. I served as project director of the symposium, and I am grateful to a number of colleagues and most especially to Professor Lester D. Stephens, head of the Department of History. Professor Thomas G. Dyer, who chaired the Bicentennial celebration, contributed enormously to the success of the symposium. The Georgia Endowment for the Humanities and the National Endowment for the Humanities provided funding for the event, as did the Georgia Athletic Association. Dr. Mary R. Baine of the Georgia Center for Continuing Education and Dr. Ronald E. Benson, executive director of the Georgia Endowment for the Humanities, contributed vitally to arrangements and planning. Most of all, I am indebted to Morraine Matthews Bartley.

Numan V. Bartley

Introduction

The popular stereotype of the American South has passed through a remarkable series of transformations during the twentieth century. In the 1920s the region was a "benighted South" of monkey trials and violence. It was, in H. L. Mencken's often-quoted phrase, "the Sahara of the Bozart," a land "almost as sterile, artistically, intellectually, culturally, as the Sahara Desert." During the depression of the 1930s the South became the nation's No. 1 economic problem, a region that, in Arthur F. Raper's words, was characterized by "depleted soil, shoddy livestock, inadequate farm equipment, crude agricultural practices, crippled institutions, a defeated and impoverished people." The profound economic impact of World War II encouraged southern state governments to pursue industrial development more vigorously and led to a partially successful effort to depict the South as the nation's No. 1 economic opportunity. Such promotional efforts continued throughout the post–World War II era, but by the late 1950s white resistance to racial desegregation had once again reduced the South to a region of violence, ignorance, and intolerance. With much of its political leadership publicly agreeing with Alabama Governor George C. Wallace's demand for "segregation now, segregation tomorrow, segregation forever," the South found itself back in its accustomed role as national stepchild. When the South did desegregate, following the 1964 civil rights law, southern whites adjusted to the change, opening the way for a politics of moderation and ultimately, in the mid-1970s, for the emergence of the Sun Belt South. The image became, as Fred Hobson pointed out, "what one might call a superior South—a region cleaner, less crowded, and more open and honest, more genuinely religious and friendly, and suddenly more racially tolerant than any other American region."

These bewildering shifts in popular imagery contributed to an abiding scholarly interest in the region. "Of books about the South, there is no end," V. O. Key prophetically observed in 1949. "Nor will there be," Key added, "so long as the South remains the region with the most distinctive

ix

character and tradition." This question of the nature and extent of southern distinctiveness has been a central concern of scholarship about the
region. White southern resistance to changes in race relations during the
1950s and 1960s occurred at a time when economic and demographic
changes made the South statistically more similar to the rest of the nation
and thereby made regional behavior appear particularly distinctive.
Books, articles, and frequent scholarly symposia grappled with what
David M. Potter labeled "the enigma of the South" and sought to unravel
the riddle of America's sphinx. Academic fascination with the region gen-
erated an important body of scholarship, but it failed to discover a con-
vincing central theme that would account for southern historical distinctiveness.

Comparative studies of slavery ultimately contributed to reorienting
the focus of scholarship. By comparing the antebellum South with other
slaveholding societies (especially Brazil), these works shifted attention
away from the question of southern distinctiveness within the United
States. Similarly, studies of southern slave communities introduced more
sophisticated approaches to the social history of the region. The widely
proclaimed birth of the Sun Belt South in the mid-1970s tended to reinforce these interpretive tendencies. With popular literature stressing the
presumed similarity between South Carolina and Southern California, the
uniqueness of the South no longer appeared to be a pressing issue. Northerners seemingly lost what William Faulkner once described as an "almost hopeless capacity and eagerness to believe anything about the South
not even provided it be derogatory but merely bizarre enough and strange
enough," and southern scholarship reached a new level of maturity, evi-
dencing a greater inclination to analyze the region on its own terms.

The essays in this volume exemplify contemporary trends in the writing
of southern history. They range over a variety of subjects, but in general
all are concerned with the shaping of southern culture. Originally delivered as papers at a symposium at the University of Georgia, the essays
examine crucial forces that molded "the southern way of life" as well as
alternative visions that failed to do so. None of the authors deals specifically with the question of southern distinctiveness within the United
States, although the essays do suggest that southern problems have increasingly become the problems that confront Americans generally. The
South ultimately achieved the economic growth that made it a part of the
Sun Belt phenomena, but, as Paul K. Conkin observes in the concluding
essay, the region's people paid a substantial price for "progress."

Immanuel Wallerstein, author of the first essay in the volume, raises the
imminently appropriate question of whether "there is a cultural entity we

may call the South." Wallerstein concludes from a survey of literature about the South that "culture turns out to be less an analytic concept or analytic construct than a rhetorical flag around which one rallies." Accepting this definition, he examines the South from a world-systems perspective and argues that "the dominant economic forces in this agricultural export region" found it necessary in the nineteenth century "to create a cultural entity known as the South." Defeat in the Civil War altered the definition of southern culture, but not until the post–World War II era did it begin "to disappear as a construct." By viewing southern culture as a product of the region's position in the world capitalist economy, Wallerstein's analysis focuses on fundamental forces that shaped southern development.

Eugene D. Genovese and Elizabeth Fox-Genovese agree that "the Old South arose and matured in direct submission to the powers of the world market," but their emphasis is on developments within the South, and specifically on the importance of religion in defining the moral base of a southern ideology. "Slavery," the authors write, "laid the foundation for a remarkably broad regional culture, manifested in an increasingly coherent and religiously grounded world view that united the slaveholders on fundamental values and linked them, if precariously, to the nonslaveholders." While stressing the point that the South's religious culture was solidly grounded in the social relations of plantation agriculture, Genovese and Fox-Genovese take southern theologians seriously and insist that their defense of slavery was not the result of political pressure, weakness, or bad faith. Although these theologians struggled with the dilemmas posed by slavery, they did succeed in constructing "a broad scriptural interpretation of society and history." The South's religious culture, the authors suggest, reached its apex in the antebellum era and thereafter retreated steadily before the onslaught of marketplace values.

In a previous work entitled *Nothing But Freedom,* Eric Foner called attention to the fact that "the United States was the only society where the freed slaves, within a few years of emancipation, enjoyed full political rights and a real measure of political power." Black southerners first exercised their newly acquired franchise in the election of delegates to state constitutional conventions. In his essay in this volume, Foner analyzes the Reconstruction conventions in which blacks for the first time participated with whites in lawmaking assemblies. "The makeup and proceedings of these conventions," he observes, "revealed a subtle interplay of politics and ideology as the [Republican] party attempted to come to terms with the aftermath of war and emancipation, satisfy its diverse constituencies, and establish a permanent place for itself on the now transformed landscape of southern politics." The bold experiment was unsuccessful. Foner says the constitutions "failed to satisfy black economic aspirations," but they did introduce sufficient political changes to unite "the bulk of the region's traditional leadership . . . in opposition."

In her essay Nell Irvin Painter examines the interrelationship of race, class, and gender in the making of the post-Reconstruction South. "What racism did in the South after the Civil War," Painter writes, "was further to imbed class relations into the etiquette of race relations." Gender was crucial to the maintenance of class relationships, she says. "Sex was the whip that white supremacists used to reinforce white solidarity, and sex was probably the only whip that would cut deeply enough to keep poor whites in line." White southern elites manipulated the potent combination of race and gender to establish economic and political control over the black and white southern underclass, Painter continues, but the social and cultural pathology of the South extended beyond "the right of the privileged to exploit the poor" to encompass a "pornographic power" wherein "the rituals of riots and lynchings [served] as reaffirmations of community values." Although pornographic power, which rested on the assumed legitimacy of racial domination, decayed during the twentieth century, white supremacists did much to shape the evolution of southern culture, Painter suggests, by creating a white southern nationalism that united whites of all classes behind issues based on race and gender.

A number of scholars including George M. Fredrickson have compared the historical evolution of race relations in the American South and in South Africa. In his essay in this volume, Fredrickson reexamines racial developments in the two areas and especially the role of the state in establishing and maintaining racial dominance. Around the turn of the twentieth century, he says, both the South and South Africa endorsed segregation "as a general label for new policies of state-enforced discrimination." White supremacists in both cases stressed "the horizontal aspects of segregation" and deemphasized "its role in maintaining a vertical racial order" that ensured white domination. Yet despite significant similarities in the racial conventions of the South and South Africa, Fredrickson focuses his analysis on the crucial differences between the two. He notes "the revolutionary change in the legal-political context of American race relations brought about by the Civil War" and the absence of "a similar watershed" in South Africa. No matter how ineffectively enforced, the Fourteenth and Fifteenth amendments placed the United States Constitution in sharp contrast to the South African Constitution of 1910, which was an "unambiguous mandate for white supremacy." In the South the black civil rights movement, the national corporate economy, the federal government, and declining fears among white southern elites that blacks would ally with lower-income whites to promote radical policies all contributed to "a reformist solution" to southern racial problems. Such an alternative, Fredrickson believes, is highly unlikely in South Africa.

Whatever the extent of racial conflict in southern culture, the interaction between Afro-Americans and transplanted Europeans in the South has been fundamental to the creation of southern culture. In his subtle analysis of Margaret Mitchell and *Gone With the Wind*, Joel Williamson suggests the extent to which Mitchell's novel embodies black culture within a white context. *Gone With the Wind* is devoid of fully developed black characters, but black culture is an important influence on whites. "Margaret Mitchell wrote a strikingly white novel," Williamson observes, "so white in fact that some of the white characters seem black." Rhett Butler, with his dark coloring and his attitudes toward work and sex, is the most significant example. Williamson examines Mitchell's childhood in a society permeated with white supremacy and racial hysteria and her earlier unpublished novella, which featured a handsome mulatto man and his white lover. Against this background, the absence of significant black characters in *Gone With the Wind* is something of a paradox, one that Williamson resolves at least in part by inquiring: "How black was Rhett Butler?" Beyond that, he raises the question: How black are white southerners generally?

Slave societies have historically extolled honor as a central cultural virtue, and the antebellum South was no exception. Southern whites cultivated honor in contrast to the presumed lack of honor among slaves. Bertram Wyatt-Brown has observed: "Honor, not conscience, shame, not guilt, were the psychological and social underpinnings of Southern culture." In his essay in this volume, Wyatt-Brown surveys the evolution of "heroes' honor" in southern literature, and particularly the decline and eventual collapse of the honorific tradition during the twentieth century. By the 1920s the South "had reached the point when searching commentary upon the dying code was possible." Honor, Wyatt-Brown states, was the major target of the probing literature produced by the Faulkner generation of southern writers. Thereafter, the "classic themes of tension between a well-defined but decadent ethical system and a shiny, corrupt, and flabby modern one . . . dissolved." By the 1970s honor was no longer "regretted or even cursed" in southern literature. "Quite unmistakably," Wyatt-Brown concludes, "the theme of honor has run its course." Modern southern writers had become increasingly absorbed in the existential problems that concern American authors generally.

The post–World War I generation of southern writers became absorbed in a reconsideration of regional values, but few were as frankly reactionary as the southern agrarians. In the final essay in the volume, Paul K. Conkin examines the agrarian critique of corporate capitalism during the 1930s. In the introduction to *I'll Take My Stand,* John Crowe Ransom condemned "industrialism," wherein "the main victims are the alienated workers, those who groan under the system, who have no intrinsic involvement with the ends of work, who suffer from insecurity and a harried, even frantic industrial regimen, who know only the brutalizing effects and none of the joys of work, and who gain only the satisfaction of an almost mindless consumption." During the depression years the agrarians attempted to develop an alternative to economic modernization and became more radical in their analyses, adopting a distributionist program and establishing themselves as "true agrarians." Ultimately, the "intellectual openness of the early thirties," Conkin observes, "gave way to the orthodoxy of a regulatory-welfare state." An industrializing South paid little heed to the agrarian argument. As one despairing agrarian suggested, "Without a realistic chance of regaining prosperity, most Americans will continue to vote for policies that maintain them as well-fed hirelings." Conkin perhaps speaks for many of us when he adds: "As one of those who so votes, I cannot help but feel a twinge of guilt." The South became a part of the Sun Belt phenomenon, but from the perspective of the agrarian critique, the region traded its soul in exchange.

If history serves as an appropriate guide, the stereotype of a Sun Belt South, in which the "southern way of life" with its overtones of segregation and hierarchy has been replaced by the "southern style of life" with its year-round golf games and barbecue cookouts, is apt to be short-lived. And again, if history can be considered suggestive, further changes in the national image of the South are likely to generate new scholarly concerns.

The University of Georgia symposium that produced this volume was designed to bring together some of America's most distinguished historians to view broadly southern history. In a sense, the volume represents the best of southern scholarship in the mid-1980s.

NUMAN V. BARTLEY

The Evolution of Southern Culture

What Can One Mean by Southern Culture?

Immanuel Wallerstein

In his famous book *The Mind of the South,* published in 1941, W. J. Cash observes: "There exists among us by ordinary [people]—both North and South—a profound conviction that the South is another land, sharply differentiated from the rest of the American nation, and exhibiting within itself a remarkable homogeneity. As to what its singularity may consist in, there is, of course, much conflict of opinion, and especially between Northerner and Southerner. But that it is different and that it is solid—on these things nearly everybody is agreed."[1]

Cash goes on to say that "if it can be said there are many Souths, the fact remains that there is also one South."[2] This is the proposition I wish to consider: that there is a cultural entity we may call the South. I shall not be concerned with what this culture is supposed to be, but whether and in what sense it is meaningful to suggest that it exists.

I feel somewhat like Michael O'Brien, who, in the introduction to his book *The Idea of the American South, 1920–1941,* thought it imperative to note at the outset:

> But it may be wise to caution the reader, especially if he be a Southerner, that the outsider feels no partisanship on the competing moral claims of these various versions of Southern identity; that is a private debate, on which it would be impertinent to intrude. To him, the debate is an interesting problem in intellectual history rather than a matter of social passion projected into history. To him, it does not matter personally whether Southerners are racist baboons or the true heirs of Aristotle, but he is intrigued by how such opinions should have come to pass.[3]

Well, not quite. It does matter to me, but for the moment I put this concern aside.

I

O'Brien discusses the controversies among analysts and the zigzag of emphasis between social and intellectual history, noting:

> There are great, and complicated, controversies among students of human consciousness and myth that the Southern historian is now obliged to address. Defining what is myth, what is "reality," and where myth can be disentangled from intellectual traditions of perception is not easy. To reduce the difficult to the simple, he is obliged to take up a position in an old dispute: that between philosophical idealism and positivism. In Southern terms, this is a choice between seeing the South itself as an idea, used to organize and comprehend disparate facts of social reality, or viewing the South as a solid and integrated social reality about which there have been disparate ideas.[4]

Since I consider myself neither a philosophical idealist nor a positivist, this choice leaves me somewhat bewildered. It is quite clear the South has been an idea. One has but to note the very large number of books which discuss that "idea" to verify this. It seems likely that the South has been a social reality, if only because there once was an entity called the Confederate States of America, willed into existence, enjoying widespread social support, and destroyed only by the force of arms. But a "solid and integrated" social reality? That depends on what we mean by such adjectives.

The concept of culture has a long and checkered past. Etymologically, it derives from the Latin verb *colere,* meaning "to till (the soil)." This root is found in words like *cultivate* and *agriculture* as well. Hence, the word *culture* has had from the beginning the implication of something that grows—and not spontaneously, but as the result of human will. Yet it is frequently used to designate phenomena that are quite the opposite of products of human will. In the literature on economic development, it is used by many as an explanation of why, despite presumably manipulable variables of economic policy, some regions of the world develop more slowly than others. For example, an economist from the South, William Nicholls, noted what he considered to be the anomaly that upper East Tennessee "developed" earlier and more rapidly than other parts of the South. He was puzzled by this. "I was forced to turn to largely noneconomic factors, related to this area's markedly different cultural tradition, for a plausible explanation."[5] Thus culture in some sense was defying will.

There is another ambiguity in the use of the word *culture.* As anthropologists have tended to use the term, *culture* is the property of a whole "people." However, in more popular parlance, *culture* refers to particular cultural behavior with regard to the arts, the manners of everyday life, etc., and is usually the property of only some members of the "people." We can get around this ambiguity by calling the latter *high culture*, but this points to a problem. It seems that within a "people" there may be several cultures—a high culture; a low culture; a culture for each class; a culture for each group as defined by religion, language, race, geographic origin of ancestors, etc. In recent decades we have been calling the latter subgroups "ethnic groups" and this practice has now been extended to the South as an American subgroup in such a book as George Brown Tindall's *The Ethnic Southerners*.

There is still another semantic problem of long standing, the relationship of the terms *culture* and *civilization*. In some usages, they are more or less synonymous. For example, Clement Eaton entitled his work on southern culture *The Waning of the Old South Civilization, 1860's–1880's*. For some other writers, however, the two terms are contrasted, as in *(folk) culture* versus *(high) civilization*. And to compound the looseness, for some, mostly non-English, usages, *civilization* refers to the everyday phenomena while *culture* refers to the highbrow. There is no consistency whatsoever, as any look at the synthetic essays in encyclopedias will reveal. Finally, there is the ambiguity between the use of *culture* (singular) and *cultures* (plural), *civilization* (singular) and *civilizations* (plural).[6]

It will be of little use to engage here in one more definitional exercise. What may be of some use, however, is to discuss the utility of the concept in any guise. I will begin by simply reporting on some of the ways this concept has been used in relation to the South. There seem to me at least three principal ways in which writings on the South have utilized the concept (but of course not writings on the South alone). These three usages have different implications for action.

First, there is culture as a description of a set of traits, culture as "tradition." By culture in this sense is meant some summum of institutions and ideas/values that is thought to be long-existing and highly resistant to change. This can be seen as a very negative thing as in Nicholls: "It has become my firm conviction that the South must choose between tradition and progress." For Nicholls, the South is an underdeveloped country (or was, at least, in 1960) with an "agrarian value system." High resistance to change of course does not mean imperviousness to change. Nicholls, for example, argues: "Within limits it would be more appropriate to argue that the South has persisted in its agrarian value system because of its lag in industrialization rather than to attribute the latter to its stubborn agrarianism."[7] The practical implication of this is clear. Industrialize, and the benighted tradition will disappear.

3

Tindall, by contrast, presents tradition more positively:

> In this perspective a larger southernism is an unquestionable reality, especially to those who have grown up in the South, and the historian can list some of the objective factors that produced it: a distinctive historical experience involving defeat and poverty; the climate and physical setting with their effects on life, tempo, emotion, and character; the presence of the Negro and his pervasive influence on the whole life of the region; the powerful religious heritage and the knowledge of good and evil; and finally, the persistence of an essentially rural culture with its neighborliness in human relations.

The practical implications are once again quite clear. Tindall is, to be sure, no stick-in-the-mud. He hopes for many kinds of changes: "Wide vistas of opportunity beckon at last, and if a leadership can emerge with the genius to seize the day, the South can exploit a chance that comes to few generations. Reconciliation is not out of reach, the land remains relatively unspoiled, the political system is more open and unrestricted than ever before. It may be something of a cliche now, but it is also a self-evident truth, that a region so late in developing has a chance to learn from the mistakes of others."

But the sagacity of a historian conversant with the power of tradition leads him to be skeptical and therefore to warn his readers, in the closing words of his essay: "But before this begins to sound like Henry Grady warmed over and spiced up with a dash of Pollyanna, let us not forget that if experience is any guide, the South will blow it. We will have to make the same mistakes all over again, and we will achieve the urban blight, the crowding, the traffic jams, the slums, the ghettos, the pollution, the frenzy, and all the other ills that modern man is heir to. We are already well on the way."[8]

What should be noted about this idea of culture as a bundle of traits, culture as a tradition, is that it forces one's vision inward. There is some entity we may call the South; it has traits; it has alternatives (either to persist in these traits or to change them); the likelihood of change may be estimated; the desirability of change may be argued; the ultimate moral responsibility lies with the entity.

There is an elementary difficulty with this approach that Richard Current has pointed out: "The South may be eternal, but what 'the South' means is not always clear. Even its boundaries are uncertain."[9] But this difficulty can be handled within the approach as an empirical question. Let us, the scholars, be more precise in our definitions and in our research. We will arrive eventually at a more careful bounding of the entity in question, one that obtains a greater consensus among scholars. The limitations of the use of the concept lie, therefore, not in the concept itself but in its less than optimal manipulations by the analysts.

A second usage of culture in the literature is quite different. Culture represents one-half of a basic human antinomy, that between mind and body, God and Mammon, good and evil. Richard Weaver makes this most explicit in the introduction to his book *The Southern Tradition at Bay:* "I expect to speak of the South therefore as a minority within the nation, whose claim to attention lies not in its success in impressing its ideals upon the nation or the world, but in something I shall insist is higher—an ethical claim which can be described only in terms of the *mandate of civilization.* In its battle for survival the South has lost ground, but it has kept from extinction some things whose value is emphasized by the disintegration of the modern world."[10] The same view appears less personally, more indirectly, in F. Garvin Davenport's discussion of southern history as a "regional myth" that has served national needs—that is, as someone else's myth. In discussing the nineteenth-century version of this myth, he says:

> The imaginative history of the post-Reconstruction period of the South is directly related to the central body of myths by which the national community defined itself in the nineteenth century. Henry Nash Smith has noted that most Americans defined the distinctive national uniqueness which separated them from Europe in terms of a nature-vs.-civilization dichotomy. The United States represented a state of nature, while the Old World represented historical civilization. Thomas Jefferson believed that the majority of Americans, because they were yeoman farmers, could be free individuals—free from restraint by social institutions or traditions; free to live in harmony with nature's laws. This meant, for Jefferson, that Americans, unlike Europeans, could live in a state of innocence rather than corruption because power would be virtually absent from a community of free and equal men. In such a social and economic condition, there would be no rulers and no ruled. . . .
>
> The democratic yeoman farmer, therefore, became the symbol of the ideal American citizen. And it was against that ideal that the myth of the Southern Cavalier was contrasted. Yeoman vs. Cavalier represented democrat vs. aristocrat, nature vs. civilization, American culture vs. European, innocence vs. corruption. Ultimately these symbols seemed to find dramatic confirmation in the Civil War when the yeoman democracy of the North, according to national mythology, successfully defended national innocence against the conspiratorial effort of the undemocratic Cavaliers to impose the corruption of the institution of slavery on the entire nation. It was viewed as a righteous war led by the yeoman figure Abraham Lincoln against the sinister plans of the Cavalier, Jefferson Davis.

5

Davenport sees the southern agrarians as retaining the mythical story and simply inverting the cast of characters:

> For while the Agrarians were participating in the continuing national quest for a rehabilitation of agrarian innocence and simplicity, they professed a regional uniqueness. . . . The South was the America of Jeffersonian ideals and eighteenth-century agrarianism. . . .
>
> This Old South, of which the twentieth-century South is the only remaining manifestation, was seen as a land of small farmers and planters, each group serving as a force of moderation on the other. The aristocratic element kept the democratic element from becoming too acquisitive, either politically or economically. The democratic element returned this same favor and, presumably, also helped to keep the aristocrats from becoming too removed from the virtue-giving soil. Civilization modified the materialism of the frontier; the frontier in turn shed its democratic spirit on civilization.[11]

In this kind of analysis, culture does not refer to the traits of a group but to those of a minority, almost inevitably a beleaguered minority, within some larger whole. This minority could be a regional minority, a class minority, an ethnic minority. Culture as virtue—that is, culture as anti-barbarism—turns out to be much more hidebound in its implications than culture as tradition. Traditions may be less than perfect. There are times and ways in which traditions ought to be changed. But virtue can only be defended. This is the explanation of Tindall's correct observation: "The belief that the South is forever disappearing has a long and honored tradition."[12]

There is a third way to discuss culture: as the expression of a binary relation. South is the counterpart of North. They are defined in relation to each other. This comes out in the almost antithetical titles of two books, John Egerton's *The Americanization of Dixie: The Southernization of America* and Richard Current's *Northernizing the South*. Both books see this binary relationship as changing over time and coming in some sense to an end, something not necessarily positive for either author.

What Egerton means can be seen in his epitaph. He quotes Malcolm X ("As far as I am concerned, [the South] is anywhere south of the Canadian border") and then a Ku Klux Klansman ("The South is going to die . . . [the South is] going the way of the rest of the country"). He concludes his book on this plaintive note: "The South, no less than the nation as a whole, is under the influence of neo-elitism and assimilation, being pulled both toward fragmentation and toward homogenization. If there is a middle ground, an integration of cultures that thrives on both unity and diver-

6

sity, that exalts both relationships and differences, it is not very much in evidence."[13]

Current sees this "Americanization of Dixie" in a somethat more positive light than Egerton. He observes that there have been many different analyses of the ways in which the South has been northernized: "Whatever the process, the result to be anticipated has been, in reality, not so much a South resembling the North as a South conforming to the modern world. Northernization has generally been synonymous with modernization." Nonetheless, he too ends his book on a plaintive note: "And so, after two hundred years, the idea of Northernizing the South, as a project to be either welcomed or resisted, continued to live on. Whether the South itself still lived on—the South as a basically and truly distinct entity—was another question."[14]

On closer look, culture as a reflection of a binary relationship may turn out to be nothing but a variant of culture as the efforts of a minority defending virtue, seeking to hold back the tide of homogenization which is reduction, corruption, the return to the lowest common denominator.

For all of these writers, without exception it seems, culture represents a problem, a concern, a moral element. Culture turns out to be less an analytic concept or analytic construct than a rhetorical flag around which one rallies, a weapon in the larger political battles. This use of the concept of culture as shorthand for a political program is not about to disappear, in the South or anywhere else. But unless we distance ourselves from it just a bit, our vision of social reality risks being obscured. I should like, therefore, to attempt to see how the rhetoric is created and why it is treated as "culture."

Let me start with one more quote. In his book *Social Origins of Dictatorship and Democracy,* Barrington Moore writes: "The South had [prior to 1865] a capitalist civilization, then, but hardly a bourgeois one."[15] While in some sense I can discern what Moore is talking about, I cannot imagine a more infelicitous and misleading way of talking about it. Since, however, Moore's formulation is in many ways typical of almost all such statements (in form, not of course in content), allow me to dissect it. It hinges around the implicit assumption that there is a smaller entity, the South, and a larger one which Moore does not name but which I call the capitalist world-economy. When he says the South had a capitalist civilization, he refers to its participation in this larger entity, which means that people in the South were subject to certain structural constraints and therefore operated within the norms of a "capitalist civilization." When he says the South did not have a "bourgeois civilization," he means that the sociopolitical influence of urban industrialists and merchants was relatively less than that of large landowners in this particular part of the world-economy. Both statements are surely true of the antebellum South. But if capitalism is a system in which the bourgeoisie dominate the social arena, the distinction between capitalist civilization and bourgeois civilization makes no sense. It only seems plausible by attributing to both the larger entity and the smaller geographical entity distinctive "cultures" despite the fact that the one encompasses the other.

Of course, as soon as we allot "cultures" to entities within entities, there is no logical end. The West has a culture, the United States has a culture, the South has a culture, Georgia has a culture, and I suppose Atlanta has a culture. In addition, blacks and whites in Georgia/the South/the United States have distinct cultures. And so on. Why not each community, each kin network, each household? And why not each generation of each group? The answer is there is no reason why not, and people do speak of cultures at each of these levels. Can we then assume each of these cultures represents some kind of enduring set of behaviors and values that is resistant to change? We can if we want to, but where does that get us?

As soon as we look closely at the smaller-scale entities, we become very conscious of how constantly changing are the sets of practices and values of small groups—within an individual's lifetime, not to speak of over longer periods, and whenever a group or an individual finds itself in a different location.

Furthermore, we know that even if group values remain constant over any period of time, we can never assume that all individuals in that group either affirm those values or engage in behavior consonant with them. At most, the statement of group values is a statistical mean of specific ways of behaving or of professed beliefs with a presumably low standard deviation. As to this presumption, we have in practice virtually zero hard evidence. Perhaps the standard deviation varies from group to group, from time to time. Perhaps? All too probably.

In what is clearly a maelstrom of constantly varying behavior, does it make sense to assume that constancy is the norm and that it is change which is to be explained? Would it not be far more defensible intellectually to assume that variability is the norm and that continuities are to be explained? If so, then perhaps we should set aside the very term *culture* as having quite misleading implications.

What we can say is that all historical systems have structures, and rules/norms/values corresponding to these structures, which are part of their operation. These structures always include some kinds of mechanisms that partially constrain deviance in some fashion. Such a historical system is, for example, the capitalist world-economy, which has its history, its changing spatial boundaries, its culture or "civilization" if you will.

Since this system has a structure that is hierarchical and involves variegated and often spatially distinct groups, the politics of this world-system involves the efforts of these multiple groups (whose existence is the result of a combination of self-definition and other-definition) in struggles over benefits. One of the ways in which groups struggle is by seeking to impose norms and behavioral practices on their members, with middling degrees of success.

Since the world-system is continuously changing, the position and definition of these groups is continuously changing. Hence the "local cultural definitions" that groups find useful is continuously changing. How, then, has it been possible in such a system to talk of things like "the mind of the South"? It has been possible because groups, in seeking to pursue their interests, will be more able to do so insofar as they can persuade their "members" to act in the present in some unified fashion. And a crucial mode of persuading these individuals, who in fact hold multiple group memberships (and hence, from the point of view of any particular group within which they are defined as falling, are individuals of divergent interests), is to persuade these individuals that the desired behavior is normal, "traditional," hallowed by time and therefore expected in the present. The re-creation of an ever-varying tradition requires the spread of the belief that no change has in fact occurred.

What we have been calling the culture of a group—say, for example, that of the South—is thus something far more fluid *and flexible* than our collective discussion heretofore has made it out to be. Each writer, each "spokesman," each orator is seeking, when he talks of this "culture," to create it as a set of rules and priorities. In the process of doing this, he claims longevity and pervasiveness as the cachet of his version of the culture. To the extent that his efforts are consonant with those of some others, he thereby creates a momentary theoretical justification of actions in the present. This is why still other persons are always in the business of reanalyzing and debunking any statement of the key features of this so-called culture. The extent of the debate that has gone on in the South about its "mind," about the boundaries of the very South that is supposed to have a mind, is in fact not significantly different from comparable debates everywhere else within the time-space boundaries of the capitalist world-economy. There is nothing special about the claim to be special. There is nothing unusual about the ambiguities surrounding all the

9

claims. The claim to specialness is part of the world-systemic political game, and it plays a central role in the operation of the system.

Interpreting the specific content of the successive claims requires looking at the evolving position of particular geographic zones in the developing world-system. For example, it seems to me, without in any sense claiming expertise in southern history, that the South and therefore its "mind," its "culture," its "civilization" has changed drastically at least several times over the past 350 years.

Before the American Revolution, was there really anything much to be called "the South"? There were juridically a set of British colonies, which were agricultural-exporting peripheral zones of the world-economy, using a good deal of coerced cash-crop labor. On a world scale, their economic role was not that different from many other such zones at the time—not only some Caribbean islands and Brazil, which are often referred to as comparable areas, but Quebec, Andalusia, Sicily, Poland, and Hungary among others. If one takes a close look at the cultures of these zones, the features which make them different at that time among themselves (and there are of course many—language, dominant religion, historical origins of their local structures, etc.) pale before the striking similarities of the attitudes we asssociate with "plantation" or "seignorial" zones in the capitalist world-economy. What we usually think of as feudal values—the combination of the harsh exploitation of labor with paternalism—is in fact less a picture of Europe in the Middle Ages than of these "plantation" zones of the capitalist world-economy.

The basic economic situation did not change after the American Revolution. If anything, the invention of the cotton gin reinforced the pattern. What changed was a theoretically accidental phenomenon. The southern states found themselves part of the United States, a sovereign state which contained other zones of differing economic role, and in which they were numerically a minority. To pursue their interests, the dominant economic forces in this agricultural export region had to create a cultural entity known as the South. It was an essential weapon. The development of U.S. nationalism led quite logically, given the situation, to the development of southern nationalism. As John McCardell correctly noted, this nationalism, "as a political movement, did require the exploitation of the proslavery argument."[16] More than that, it required the sense that there were within this one political entity "two distinct peoples, two distinct civilizations, one in the North and the other in the South."[17] I am not saying that the Civil War was inevitable; this would be absurd. What I am saying is that it was not at all surprising given the ways in which the capitalist world-economy operates, and it was not at all exceptional. And

I am also saying that the concept of the Old South was a construct useful to many in the world political conflicts of the time. The Old South was in some sense created as a mental construct only a short time before it was historically eliminated as a material construct.

The defeat of the Confederacy changed all that, and most of all culturally. The U.S. federal state thereafter pursued energetically an economic and political policy geared to transforming the role of the United States in the world-economy. This federal state was not particularly anxious to change too much in how the South operated locally, at least in the following fifty to seventy-five years. Yes, Reconstruction and carpetbagging were traumas from the point of view of many persons in the South. But they changed less than we often argue. What they changed most was how the South thought of itself—that is, what political line it was going to follow.

Clearly the old line hadn't worked and had to be shed. Basically two new lines were put forward and their proponents fought for supremacy. On the one hand, there was the line of the New South. The New South was the path of cultural assimilation. It was no different than a hundred variants we see across the globe. Advocates of the New South essentially said that if "we" are behind, it is because "we" are outdated—technologically, to be sure; culturally, at least in part. Let us therefore modify our ways, retaining nonetheless some label so as to make a political claim for "aid," and we will catch up.

The other possible line was that of the southern agrarians. Catch up to what? was their watchword. We are conceding everything of value in the effort to "catch up," which, even if we try, will never really succeed. Even at the end of the horizon, there will be no true material equality, and our quality of life will have disappeared. Once again, this kind of claim to particularistic "agrarian" virtue has been put forward in every zone of the world-economy undergoing an intensification of its peripheralization.

I am not here to mediate between the proponents of the New South and the southern agrarians. They are both dead-end positions, and they are also the only two that were really available. What I wish to insist upon is that they were both very different from the Old South and were both claims to create a "culture"—claims at best only partially realized. Neither the New South nor the agrarian ideal swept the other from the scene and became the true, the only culture of the South.

When the United States moved into its position as unquestioning world hegemonic power as of 1945, all changed again. It was no longer in the interest of the dominant political forces of the U.S. federal state to have a "backward" geographical zone, just as it was no longer in its interest to have the denial of political rights to minorities such as the blacks. The homogenization of America was an urgent political (and diplomatic) need of the U.S. federal state. The industrialization of the South and the Civil Rights Act were all part of a larger picture of "cultural" reorganization. The question was only how various subgroups would react to it. Blacks in the U.S. reacted by asserting, in many ways for the first time, their separate "culture." This is easy to explain, but not our subject here. The South reacted to it, it seems to me, largely by beginning to disappear as a construct.

Perhaps you will not think this is so, and this very forum may be negative evidence—or it may be an effort to stem the tide. Of course, there are people in whose interests it would be to stem that particular tide, but surely not, for example, most of those who have become active in the Republican party, part of whose effort has been for the last thirty years the redrawing of U.S. cultural regional boundaries. This is what they mean by constantly referring to the "new majority." Egerton put forward the argument in 1974 that "it is mostly Southerners with a particular perspective—for want of a better term, it is Southern liberals—who still gather to talk introspectively about their region."[18] One can see why this might be so.

And now that the United States is entering its posthegemonic phase (despite Mr. Reagan's Canutelike efforts to order the ocean to recede), will there be a place for a southern mind? Perhaps, but if so, of a very different kind. The decades ahead for the United States are probably decades of increasing internal struggle as the nation adjusts with difficulty to its slow economic and hence geopolitical decline in the world-system. For many Americans this will be the opportunity for new or renewed egalitarian claims; for others, this decline holds the promise of great short-term programs of enrichment.

Many "cultures" will be born or renewed in the decades ahead. The growing worldwide attacks on the capitalist system include attacks on the "universalist" system of values which is used to sustain it. This encourages thereby the reassertion of "particularisms." We are seeing this throughout the world. Why not the South? But also why in the South? Perhaps rather in Georgia. If we see such new particularisms, you may be surprised what traditions they may begin to invoke in the South—perhaps the ultraradical claims of some threads of early Protestantism. On a worldwide measuring scale, the South may move from being a concept towards the right of the political spectrum to being one towards the left. Or it may not.

Since culture is so fluid and so flexible, it is virtually impossible to make any sensible projections of this. We do better to make projections about the world-economy and the world political system (including the antisystemic movements found everywhere) and assume that the protagonists will make "cultural" claims whose details may vary enormously but whose utility can be analyzed. The point is that if we want to know the traditions of the near future the last place we should look is at the traditions of the near past.

Notes

1. W. J. Cash, *The Mind of the South* (New York, 1941), vii.

2. Ibid., viii.

3. Michael O'Brien, *The Idea of the American South, 1920–1941* (Baltimore, 1979), xi.

4. Ibid., xiii.

5. William H. Nicholls, *Southern Tradition and Regional Progress* (Chapel Hill, 1960).

6. I have discussed the importance of the distinction between singular and plural usage in "The Modern World-System as a Civilization" (Conference on "Civilizations and Theories of Civilizing Processes: Comparative Perspectives," University of Bielefeld, June 15–17, 1984).

7. Nicholls, *Southern Tradition and Regional Progress*, x, 18.

8. George Brown Tindall, *The Ethnic Southerners* (Baton Rouge, 1976), 86, 241.

9. Richard N. Current, *Northernizing the South* (Athens, Ga., 1983), 11.

10. Richard M. Weaver, *The Southern Tradition at Bay* (New Rochelle, 1968), 29 (italics added).

11. F. Garvin Davenport, Jr., *The Myth of Southern History: Historical Consciousness in Twentieth-Century Southern Literature* (Nashville, 1967), 7–9, 57–58.

12. Tindall, *The Ethnic Southerners*, 2. Wayne Mixon, in the introduction to Current, *Northernizing the South,* reminds us that "at the very beginning of the American nation, most of the Founding Fathers from the South not only believed that their region was distinctive but that its interests were threatened by the rest of the country" (p. ix).

13. John Egerton, *The Americanization of Dixie: The Southernization of America* (New York, 1974), 208.

14. Current, *Northernizing the South,* 12–13, 117.

15. Barrington Moore, Jr., *Social Origins of Dictatorship and Democracy: Lord and Peasant in the Making of the Modern World* (Boston, 1966), 121.

16. John McCardell, *The Idea of a Southern Nation: Southern Nationalists and Southern Nationalism, 1830–1860* (New York, 1979), 49.

17. Current, *Northernizing the South,* 17.

18. Egerton, *The Americanization of Dixie,* 15.

The Religious Ideals
of Southern Slave Society

Eugene D. Genovese and
Elizabeth Fox-Genovese

Southern conservatives have long insisted that the Old South should be understood primarily as a religious society. From the Twelve Southerners' fiery manifesto *I'll Take My Stand* through Richard Weaver's brilliant *The Southern Tradition at Bay* to the recent restatement in Fifteen Southerners, *Why the South Will Survive*, and M. E. Bradford's penetrating historical studies, conservatives have stressed the South's continuity with premodern Europe. They have argued that the fundamental values of southern culture, in contradistinction to those of northern, have been religiously grounded and have established the South as the legitimate heir of Europe's Christian civilization. In their view, the North, in contrast, has been heir to those European values that have historically represented a revolutionary rupture with, and repudiation of, Christian civilization. In this spirit Allen Tate announced that modern Europe itself had broken faith and that the only genuine Europeans left were to be found in the American South.

Hence, conservatives have dismissed slavery as—in Bradford's word—a distraction. But they cannot explain how the European traditions they admire managed to flourish in the South but not in the North, which, after all, arose out of the same transatlantic migration as part of the extraordinary expansion of European capitalism's emerging world market—as embedded in what Immanuel Wallerstein has called the world-system. And if they point to the South's long and dogged commitment to a rural way of life, we must reply that the slave plantation provided the social basis for the durability of that way of life, which has been in steady retreat ever since emancipation and the conquest of the South by the values of the marketplace. Indeed, for the evidence of that retreat during the

14

twentieth century one need only turn to the writings of these very conservatives and to such moving testimonials of such scions of the old planter aristocracy as William Alexander Percy's *Lanterns on the Levee*. For if the Old South arose and matured in direct submission to the power of the world market for which it raised vital staples, its plantation system and attendant society of extended households guaranteed that the South would develop as a society and culture in but not of the larger transatlantic capitalist world.

The conservatives' fundamentally sound and heuristically rich thesis of a specifically religious society and culture can only be sustained by lifting it from its philosophically idealist moorings and grounding it in the material reality—specifically, the social relations—of a maturing slave society. In particular, only through such a grounding can we avoid the trap into which these conservatives have fallen—that of implicitly severing the high culture of the intellectuals and educated planters from the culture of the slaveholders, big and small, as if, for example, the work of the sophisticated theologians had little or no bearing on the work of the humblest of the down-home preachers.

The distinctive religious character of antebellum southern society was directly related to slavery as a social system. Southern high culture was intimately linked to the daily beliefs and practices of both slaveholding and nonslaveholding southerners. Slavery laid the foundation for a remarkably broad regional culture, manifested in an increasingly coherent and religiously grounded view that united the slaveholders on fundamental values and linked them, if precariously, to the nonslaveholders. Southern culture, for all its regional, racial, and class variants, developed in essential respects as a piece, of which religion constituted the warp. If the theologians became, over time, more articulate and determined in their defense of slavery, and if they smothered doubts about its Christian character, they did not primarily do so under political pressure and in bad faith. The measure of truth in the familiar attribution of weakness and bad faith is outweighed by its mischief: Many of the religious leaders were too devout and too brave to prostitute themselves and the churches to which, often literally, they gave their lives. Their views resulted from their intense participation in a southern community they were shaped by and helped to shape.

Southern theologians, especially the Evangelicals, did wrestle with the egalitarian claims of their faith. The egalitarian promises of Christianity were not new to the late eighteenth and nineteenth centuries. As many Christians, not merely the members of radical sects, had long insisted, the equality of souls before God constituted an essential element of Chris-

15

tianity as a faith. But first the Catholic Church and then the Protestant, albeit somewhat more uneasily, had developed a venerable tradition of separating God's concerns from those of Caesar and of ascribing slavery to the latter. The attempt to link the ideological and political opposition to slavery as a form of labor to the concerns of God reflected a new determination to force the world to realize divine standards in its daily business. The history of that complex process provides an indispensable, if insufficiently evoked, context for the development of a distinctive southern evangelical Christianity. For southern theologians cannot be understood either as corrupt cynics who capitulated to the material interests of their congregations or as reactionaries who unquestioningly accepted traditional notions of the subordination—including ownership—of laboring people. Rather, the southern theologians as a group figured as serious and soul-searching participants in the heated and intersecting debates of their era: What should be the relation between religion and society? What should be the relation between theology and modern knowledge, from political theory to science?

Among antebellum southerners, the slaveholders in particular, religion enjoyed a privileged place as the cornerstone of shared beliefs, and from at least 1820 to the war southerners viewed Christianity as the moral foundation of their social system. Southerners, led by their theologians, turned to the Bible to sanction slavery. And the Bible served them well, for it did sanction slavery. In regularly turning to and relying upon the Bible, they rigorously defended slavery as an appropriate foundation for the good society and an appropriate model for harmonious social relations, both of which they viewed as necessarily hierarchical. They accepted much of the modern world, but they resolutely insisted that it could not survive if grounded in the social relations of "free society."

The manifold efforts to construct or reconstruct a Christian society entailed new departures. The rhetoric often suggested a project of restoration, but southern religious leaders accepted much of the modern world, which they determined to master through the conversion of both slaveholders and slaves, through the provisions of carefully controlled education, and through the reconciliation of religion with modern science. Their religious beliefs represented the social system they increasingly defended, but southern religion developed in large part as the world view of a modern slave society enmeshed in an increasingly capitalist Atlantic world. They consciously sought not merely to save individual souls but to build a Christian community. By 1820, thanks to the evangelical movement, the South had been largely re-Christianized, and the slaveholding elite was beginning to espouse religion as the anchor of its view of itself and its world.

Like southern society itself, the southern theologians' reclaiming of religion as the foundation of social values constituted something new under
the sun. For many southern theologians, especially the Evangelicals and
among them the Methodists, were troubled by the claims of spiritual
equality and their potential consequences for equality of condition in this
world. The abolitionist argument against slavery had developed from precisely the same general social conditions as the evangelical sects themselves. However imbued with Christian ideals and rhetoric, it was the
child of capitalism, and of that attendant ideology of individualism which
was making such heavy conquests in all facets of thought and society. In
this respect, its place in the development of a distinctive southern culture
can be likened to that of Jeffersonian republicanism: It had embraced a
new rhetoric and even new values but had not jettisoned a deep commitment to existing social relations. In effect, the southern theological community did seriously entertain the individualistic and egalitarian claims of
new religious currents, but in time it rejected them, or at least rejected
their extreme challenges.

The southern churches boasted able theologians. James Henley Thornwell of South Carolina, to cite the most prominent, ranked among the
ablest in the United States, arguably second to none. They are largely
forgotten now, as is generally the fate of those who back losing causes in
great wars, especially causes as offensive as slavery. Yet in their own day
the theologians were held in high regard and exercised notable influence.
In the countryside especially, the head of the household or his wife would,
from time to time, collect the family, often including the house servants,
around the fire at night and read aloud. Frequently, the text would be a
printed sermon to supplement the Bible, which retained pride of place in
the household.

At that, the influence of the theologians cannot be isolated from that of
such social theorists as George Frederick Holmes, George Fitzhugh, and
Henry Hughes, such political scientists as John C. Calhoun, Beverley
Tucker, Albert Bledsoe, and James H. Hammond, such legal scholars and
jurists as T. R. R. Cobb, George Sawyer, Thomas Ruffin, and John Belton
O'Neall. For with only occasional exceptions, these ostensibly "secular"
social, political, legal, and moral theorists carefully grounded their doctrines in Scripture, which they knew well. Virtually all took for granted
that no view of society would prevail—or deserve to prevail—unless its
divine sanction could be made evident, for their constituents took their
Christianity seriously. To put it another way, typically the intellectuals
shared the sensibility of the ordinary slaveholders, big and small, and
those who did not learned quickly to maintain pretense if they did not

17

wish to spit into the wind. Their Christian defense of slavery did not depend upon the finer points of Arminian or Calvinist doctrine. It offered a broad scriptural interpretation of society and history. Thus, the proslavery theology of the Baptist Reverend Thornton Stringfellow or the Methodist William Smith paralleled in all principal respects that of the Presbyterian James Henley Thornwell.

Stringfellow, Smith, Thornwell, and others carried the proslavery argument to new and higher ground. They advanced from theology to history and to what George Fitzhugh and Henry Hughes proclaimed in 1854 as "sociology." The defense of racial slavery passed into a general defense of slavery—of "slavery in the abstract," as Fitzhugh called it. Indeed, during the 1850s the most prominent scriptural defenses of slavery—those of George Armstrong, William Brownlow, Josiah Priest, Frederick Ross, and the especially influential John Fletcher—as well as the secular defense that invariably invoked scriptural authority, advanced, steadily if unevenly, toward some variant of the defense of slavery regardless of race, toward the argument that slavery provided the foundation of a proper, safe, Christian social order for all people.

The advance to higher ground had been proceeding for several decades. Even T. R. Dew, that erudite admirer of modernism who doubted that slavery, at least in its southern form, had a future in a world of inevitable industrialization, saw no solution to the "social question" short of some kind of subjugation of the laboring classes, white as well as black. Not every southern theorist, religious or secular, thought that chattel slavery could or should last forever, but by the 1850s the overwhelming majority thought that without some form of servitude for those laboring classes civilization would perish. To that extent Thornwell spoke for the southern intellectuals as a group in 1860: "That nonslaveholding states will eventually have to organize labour, and introduce something so like Slavery that it will be impossible to discriminate between them, or else to suffer from the most violent and disastrous insurrections against the system which perpetuates their misery, seems to be as certain as the tendencies in the laws of capital and population to produce the extremes of poverty and wealth."

The ideological consensus that emerged among the slaveholders and that linked them to the nonslaveholding yeomen left ample room for serious, even bitter, political differences between Democrats and Whigs, and even more dangerously, between secessionists and unionists. The hegemony of the slaveholders proved especially fragile during the war, when a substantial portion of the upcountry yeomen defected from the Confederacy. But the unraveling of the Confederate war effort, in its own way, demonstrated the existence of a prior consensus upon which the Confederate leaders had thought they could rely.

The consensus rested on the acceptance of slavery as a proper social system, but southerners did not rest their defense of slavery on racial grounds and simply taunt northerners and Englishmen for having their own social problems. They moved their critique toward the repudiation and condemnation of free society. As southern intellectuals felt compelled to examine their premises and beliefs, they found themselves led, step by step, to the conclusion that while a racially inferior laboring class might have to submit to chattel slavery, all laboring classes would have to submit to some form of personal servitude.

For antebellum southerners the distinctions turned less upon race and level of wealth than upon relations to farm or plantation households. Or, to put it differently, the nature of the South as a society of households and the special form of the ideology of individualism that southerners developed on the basis of that household structure and the intellectual traditions of early modern republicanism permitted southerners, however uneasily, to encompass the contradictions of their social elitism and their democratic politics. Since the southern farm or plantation household encompassed within itself relations of production as well as reproduction, southerners could, more easily than their northern counterparts, ascribe labor to the governance of the household head. Legitimate labor was contained within the household, in which it was supported and governed according to the principles of dependence. Labor that escaped household governance could plausibly be viewed as anomalous and disruptive. Under these conditions, the wide social and economic gaps between large planters and poor yeomen could be bridged, although not without tensions. In this sense, the South did constitute a "slaveholders' republic" in which republican political practice depended heavily upon its roots in slavery as a social system. No matter that most yeomen were not slaveholders. They—especially those in the plantation districts—were, by the inescapable social and economic logic of their society, potential slaveholders. And that potential—that acceptance of the legitimacy of slaveholding—guaranteed their membership in the company of male individuals who held responsibility for the governance of women, children, and laborers. The ideological consensus that bound slaveholders to nonslaveholding smallholders stopped comfortably short of the extreme defense of slavery in the abstract, but the depth and breadth of the consensus expanded in two impressive developments. The extreme view spread rapidly among the elite, and an admittedly qualified and disguised reflection of that view spread among the small propertyholders. The unraveling of the consensus, as the military needs of the Confederacy pressed unacceptably among the upcountry smallholders, forcefully revealed the foundations upon which it had rested.

The consensus we have called "ideological" was understood by its adherents to be quintessentially "moral." Southern spokesmen—and spokeswomen, too—hailed slavery as civilization's one great bulwark against anarchism, communism, socialism, Mormonism, Millerism, bloomerism, and free love. Christian values and the Christian family were crumbling throughout free society. Only the South stood firmly against all such madness. Only the South remained liberal-spirited in accordance with the modern age but intransigent against social disorder. And the proslavery ideologues were convinced that the isms grew out of infidelity, notwithstanding the hypocrisy and cant of northern divines who could not see that abolitionism was itself a defiance of God's manifest will. Even the moderate northern antislavery divines, who tried to hold themselves aloof from the abolitionists and who censured their alleged excesses, were inadvertently doing the devil's work. A Channing, a Wayland were undoubtedly honest and well-meaning, but they were nonetheless trying to dismantle the God-ordained social relations necessary to sustain a Christian community.

The abolitionists may have scored heavily in New England and among the sophisticates of the seaboard cities, but when they scored in the Burned-Over District, the Western Reserve, and the rural hinterland of the Old Northwest, their success depended upon receptivity to their biblical exegesis, flimsy as it might now seem—depended, that is, upon the ability of their ministers to win an argument politically they could not win intellectually. In the South it was no contest, for the abolitionists inadvertently fell back on the one argument guaranteed to alarm and disgust the country people and even the conservative Episcopalians of Charleston, Savannah, and Natchez.

Too often, when pressed hard in biblical exegesis, not only the radical abolitionists but the moderate antislavery men like Channing and Wayland boldly asserted that if the Bible could in fact be shown to condone slavery it would deserve to be condemned as an immoral book. This heresy removed any last doubt that the abolitionists were thinly veiled atheists, and its assertion by a Baptist minister, college president, and moral philosopher like Wayland led even moderate and conservative southerners to conclude that further discourse with northerners was fruitless. The southern rejoinder, as might be expected, was short, harsh, and to the point: If we are Christians, we believe in the divine inspiration of the Bible

20

and in its revealed Truth. God tells us what is moral and what is sinful. We do not presume to tell Him.

The southern preachers rarely harangued their congregations on the slavery question—rarely thought it necessary to take the pulpit in defense of slavery at all. They usually restricted their occasional sermons on slavery to the reciprocal duties of masters and slaves—"servants," as they preferred to call them. They dutifully and dully preached obedience and submission to the slaves, who normally seized the opportunity to catch up on their sleep. They had something more useful to say to the masters, who normally stayed awake. Slaveownership, they insisted, entailed Christian obligations, to be scorned at the risk of a master's immortal soul. The preachers thereby did their best to Christianize, humanize, soften the attitude of the masters toward their slaves, while they quietly reaffirmed the divine sanction for slavery as a social system. In the event, southerners fashioned a view of the world and of social relations that emphasized the legitimacy of slavery and of hierarchical social relations, including, first and foremost, those between men and women.

The churches played an even more important role in the lives of the rural common folk than they did in the lives of town and village elite. In particular, they dominated the schools, which at all levels were grounded in religious principles. The nonslaveholders turned to their churches for a variety of social services and to bolster the social order, including family and sexual order. In this respect the churches helped to transmit and even to enforce norms of how men should treat women, how husbands should treat wives, and how women should behave as women. Those norms differed little or not at all from the norms proposed to the slaveholders.

In much of the South the churches constituted the only public centers, except for the courthouses and local stores or taverns, and even the courthouses were taken over by the ministers for Sunday preaching. At the very moment northerners were forging those "voluntary associations" that Tocqueville identified as the mediations of a democratic and market society, rural and town southerners were still living in a world composed primarily of households that contained within themselves the basic relations of production and reproduction. This network of households did not readily generate women's associations, libraries, orphanages, and benevolent societies. Southern towns and villages lagged well behind their northern counterparts. In the rural areas and in the villages the churches sponsored and encompassed most of the social activities. They assumed responsibility for providing most social services not provided directly through households. Ministers arranged to have families take in orphaned children, and families that took the initiative before being asked were likely to be churchgoing families. Over time, some independent associations developed, especially in the towns, but the churches continued to provide the decisive impetus for women's organizations and sense of social purpose. And those organizations usually accepted male direction, especially by ministers.

The slaveholding men, but especially the women, explicitly looked to religion to provide a basic sense of community. They did not doubt the salvation of truly Christian slaves or of poor and uneducated whites. But they did know that faith could not level social distinctions, did suspect that social distinctions influenced the quality of faith, and often did assume that the difference of station on earth would somehow be reflected in Heaven. They valued the exhilarating enthusiasm of camp and protracted meetings and attended them in large numbers. Even Episcopalians turned out on occasion. They remained intrinsic to southern country and village life everywhere. Yet, for the vast majority of slaveholders, the reality of bonds among members of a Christian community never implied social equality. They became comfortable with the idea of bonds among those who were and should be unequal—bonds among the members of a hierarchical society. That was the whole point of their paternal responsibilities towards their slaves. Their assertion of Christian bonds among those who were not and should not be considered equal increasingly distinguished them from northerners, who were emphasizing equality, at least of whites, but were losing their sense of Christian bonds and responsibilities, which derived from acknowledged inequality.

The camp and protracted meetings no doubt provided special and frequently irresistible social opportunities for rural southerners of all classes who did not have ready access to diversion, but the vast majority of those who attended accepted their central religious purpose. If women came to these meetings for company and conversation, they found both in religious idiom. Especially for the Evangelicals, their "sisterhood" and "brotherhood" derived from their common experience in Christ, not simply their common experience of the human condition. The camp and protracted meetings underscored the Christian dimension of fellowship in southern society. Although men frequently met in such public arenas as the courthouse, camp and protracted meetings provided the leading occasions for large groups of families to meet. The numbers who attended far exceeded the numbers of church members, but the two groups should probably not be divided too sharply. For the frequenters of these meetings constituted a large reservoir not merely of potential church members, but of likely church attenders. Those who participated heard the most concentrated doses of preaching that the southern churches had to offer. And the preachers stressed the importance of Christian faith to full membership in southern society, stressed the bonds of southern society as the bonds of Christianity. Thus these meetings powerfully disseminated the idea of southern society as a Christian community composed of full and potential members.

The widespread southern sense of belonging to a Christian community could not have developed easily, if at all, had a spirit of religious toleration not accompanied it. For, contrary to the assertions of many historians, toleration and Christian fellowship outweighed denominational bigotry throughout the South. Of bigotry there was plenty, and if the preachers had had their way, there might have been much more. But the preachers, or the more narrowly sectarian of them, did not have their way. Their congregations hemmed them in and demanded toleration and respect for other denominations. And, contrary to another myth, the plantation districts appear to have been even more good-spirited than the cities. Many churchgoing slaveholders went twice on Sunday, often to hear, say, a Presbyterian in the morning and a Methodist in the afternoon. This interdenominational coexistence in the communities meant that a premier theologian or religious leader like Thornwell, Levi Silliman Ives, or William Smith could expect to preach to large audiences when on the road at a quarterly or synod meeting or for some other purpose. It also meant that college presidents and professors, as well as academy principals and teachers—most of whom were likely to be ministers or active church laymen—were able to reach across denominations and social classes, for their reputations as educated and important men preceded them and served them well among those country people so often disparaged as yokels in the travel accounts and scholarly literature. Southerners expected their preachers to breathe some fire and show themselves to be moved by the Spirit as well as the Book. But they also appreciated hearing the Book, which they knew well, preached at a high level.

The interdenominational cooperation of southern Christians stemmed directly from the rural character of their society and from the primordial role of the churches in assuring a common culture and social cohesion. Interdenominational cooperation went hand in glove with passionate attachment of individuals to particular churches and with frequent splits in churches over questions of discipline and theology. The discriminations mattered, sometimes deeply, to committed church members, but they primarily concerned rivalries among church members. Vis-à-vis the numerous southern Christians who did not belong to churches, church members and leaders minimized rivalries in favor of strengthening the Christian consensus.

In the absence of widespread common schools, the churches through their Sunday schools provided most of the education that the minimally educated poorer country people received. This quasi-monopoly of education assured them the ability to instill the rudiments of a Christian sensibility among broad segments of the population. Nonchurch members frequently attended church, and even more attended camp meetings. The cooperation of preachers of different denominations ensured that the non-church members could identify with a broader Christian community. The need to hold the allegiance of their nonmembers encouraged the preachers to minimize denominational quarrels, or at least to take pains to contain the community divisiveness that the sometimes intense debates might provoke.

Men and women drew from religion a model for themselves in their world. They went to church principally to hear preaching. They listened intently. They regularly noted the texts in their diaries or correspondence, often commented on the quality of the sermon and—that which was not the same thing—on the quality of the preaching, and sometimes recorded a précis of the sermon, perhaps with a statement of agreement or dissent. The Bible offered a common language through which to interpret their personal and social moral problems. It is surely significant that they did not use the Bible for telling quotations as they did use Shakespeare. The familiar language of the Bible defied the self-conscious quotation marks. And few ever questioned its relevance to daily life, including daily life with their slaves.

Precious few slaveholders, male or female, invoked religion to question the legitimacy of slavery as a social system. Those who seek to identify some distinctive female perspective on southern society may point to many women's interest in revivals as a tangible expression of shared Christian feeling and may suggest that some women minimized the conflicts inherent in their society. But the women were, if anything, quicker than their men to point to social divisions, to cut *arrivistes,* and to refuse to know or to understand whites who differed from themselves. Most women, like most men, believed that the Lord intended the social divisions of their world and had not instructed anyone to change them.

Thus, the piety and religious convictions of the women did not move them to become reformers, as was happening in the North, or even move them to significant participation in organized charity. They met their religious obligations through ministering to their own households, under-

24

stood to include their slaves. Religion had a special meaning for those who lived in a world in which epidemics, childbirth, and personal violence made death omnipresent, regularly claiming the young with the old. There is nothing more poignant in the diaries and letters of both the men and the women than their struggle to accept that most ghastly of human miseries, the death of their children. They berated themselves for having loved their children more than God, for having loved life itself, and they fought, with astonishing courage, against every temptation to question His will. Men could write of their hopes for their sons and routinely add, "if he outlives me." Premature and sudden death stalked every household and might have driven the survivors mad had they lacked faith in its sanctification.

In other respects, too, religion offered both solace and self-control in a world of omnipresent danger from weather and illness—and from other people. The slaveholders knew that their slaves could poison or assault them at any moment, but they did not live as if under a state of siege. They believed in their fitness, as well as their right and duty, to govern their slaves and to command their labor. Necessarily, they had to believe that they could be loved and revered—or at least respected—by those on whom they imposed their will. Their preachers and their Bible helped them square the circles. For the slaveholder the Christian religion, as it was intended to, defined and enforced their gender-specific lives as men and women. It addressed them as Christians but, in the very first instant, it addressed them discretely as Christian men or women. Religion offered both men and women consolation and an unmatched source of personal fortitude in the face of death, loss, and the trials of everyday life. Both men and women recognized faith as God's grace—as a privilege that had to be struggled for. Despite the efforts of the more rigid theologians, the preachers generally steered a middle course. Most invoked God's grace with sufficient ambiguity to avoid extreme Arminianism or Calvinism. The result was often theologically messy and often evoked scathing comments in the diaries of slaveholders whose understanding of "grace" and "salvation by faith" differed from that of their pastors. But here too a spirit of toleration and patience—a willingness to leave the final answers to God—usually prevailed over all calls for doctrinal purity.

Politically, institutionally, and ideologically, toleration of error in the more esoteric matters of doctrine strengthened the consensus on morals and social duty. If men were encouraged to assume responsibility for others, whom they were also obliged to govern and discipline, women were encouraged to accept governance. Northerners also sharply differentiated gender roles, but emphasized the differences less in religion, perhaps because the feminization of religion had proceeded so far that, however much religion allowed for women's values, it emphasized gender differences less and less—or it made less and less allowance for distinctive male characteristics within a Christian discourse.

The scriptural proslavery argument, like its supposedly secular variant, consisted in a self-conscious defense of particularism as a positive good. While northerners retained their own prejudices about gender and racial relations—even class relations, which they preferred not to mention at all—their intransigent commitment to universalism, understood as equality among believers, increasingly exposed their residual particularism as little more than prejudice. Southerners openly celebrated particularism. In so doing they may have violated the inner logic of Protestantism, but they forged a distinctive sensibility that wonderfully reflected the distinctive character of their own slave society.

Their personal characters reflected the distinctive character of the slave society. Slaveholders were not unique in preparing themselves to face death and bear all earthly sorrows with Christian fortitude, but that is not the point. Whatever may be said of others, their Christianity helped forge them into an unusually strong people, while it confirmed them in allegiance to their peculiar institution, and, indeed, institutions, in this world—confirmed their sense of being part of a community, a society, a world worth dying for.

The War Memorial, across from the statehouse in Columbia, South Carolina, bears the inscription: "They were willing to die." As for the slaveholders of 1861, having long since commended their souls to Christ, indeed they were.

Notes

An earlier version of this paper was delivered at a conference on "The Old South and the Conservative Tradition" held at the National Humanities Center, Research Triangle Park, North Carolina, in April 1985. We are grateful to Charles Blitzer and his excellent staff for having provided the occasion and to those colleagues who attended and offered stimulating criticism and suggestions. In particular, we should like to thank the formal panelists: Armstead L. Robinson, who presided, William Cooper, Jon Wakelyn, and Bertram Wyatt-Brown. Our generalizations are based on the research we have been doing for a book on the southern slaveholders. Our indebtedness to a wide variety of scholars of different specialties and viewpoints should be clear. When our book is ready we shall do our best to acknowledge that debt properly.

For the moment we trust we may be permitted to cite some of our own publications for those who wish an elaboration of our theoretical framework and documentation of some of the generalizations: Fox-Genovese and Genovese, *Fruits of Merchant Capital: Slavery and Bourgeois Property in the Rise and Expansion of Capitalism* (New York, 1983); Genovese and Fox-Genovese, "Slavery, Economic Development, and the Law: The Dilemma of Southern Political Economists, 1800–1860," *Washington and Lee Law Review* 41 (1984); 1–29; Fox-Genovese, "Antebellum Southern Households: A New Perspective on a Familiar Question," *Review* [The Fernand Braudel Center, SUNY–Binghamton] 7 (1984): 215–253; Fox-Genovese, *Within the Plantation Household: Black and White Women of the Old South* (Chapel Hill, forthcoming); Genovese, *"Slavery Ordained of God": The Southern Slaveholders' View of Biblical History and Modern Politics*, The Fortenbaugh Memorial Lecture (Gettysburg, 1986); Genovese, "The Southern Slaveholders' View of the Middle Ages," in *Medievalism in American Culture*, ed. Bernard Rosenthal and Paul E. Szarmach (forthcoming).

Politics and Ideology in the Shaping of Reconstruction: The Constitutional Conventions of 1867–1869

Eric Foner

In the Reconstruction Act of 1867, Congress required the states of the old Confederacy (except Tennessee, which had been readmitted to the Union in 1866) to hold conventions to draft new constitutions incorporating the principle of political equality for blacks. Thus was inaugurated a new era in southern politics. The Republican party, which had barely existed south of Mason and Dixon's line before 1867, swept to political victory in the elections to choose convention delegates. Their electoral majority united blacks seeking equal citizenship and economic autonomy, white Unionists committed to preventing a return of "rebel rule," upcountry yeomen threatened by rising indebtedness and a loss of their cherished economic independence, economic promoters who saw the party as a vehicle for the creation of a New South, and northerners for whom Reconstruction presented the opportunity to reshape southern life in the free-labor image of the North. The makeup and proceedings of these conventions revealed a subtle interplay of politics and ideology as the party attempted to come to terms with the aftermath of war and emancipation, satisfy its diverse constituencies, and establish a permanent place for itself on the now transformed landscape of southern politics.

With most antebellum officials barred from membership, and blacks and carpetbaggers representing the plantation belt, the conventions of 1867–69, as a British visitor remarked, mirrored "the mighty revolution that had taken place in America." The delegates, hostile newspapers contended, were devoid of political experience and possessed virtually "no property at all." The North itself had rarely witnessed such gatherings. Lawyers comprised two-thirds of the Illinois constitutional convention of 1870, but made up only a small fraction of the southern delegates. And, of course, blacks for the first time sat alongside whites as lawmakers, a fact that riveted the attention of southern freedmen. In parts of South Carolina, blacks refused to sign labor contracts for 1868, "expecting the convention to give them lands." When important issues came to the floor in Virginia, they crowded the galleries; tobacco factories reported mass absenteeism, and white households were forced by a lack of servants "to cook their own dinners, or content themselves with a cold lunch." Nor were blacks alone in observing the proceedings with "intense interest." From Congress came appeals for "wise and judicious action," and warnings that the completed documents must meet the approval of "the enlightened judgment of the country." To northern officeholders, complained radical carpetbagger Albion W. Tourgee, it seemed to make "no difference what may be the needs of the people in these States. The Republican party and its interests are paramount."[1]

Since most opponents of Reconstruction had abstained from voting, Democrats or Conservatives comprised a small minority of the one thousand or so delegates, and a high rate of absenteeism further reduced their influence. Generally, in the words of one black delegate, they contented themselves with assailing Republican principles "with all that bitter resentment and revenge so characteristic of a once ruling, but now waning aristocracy." Some Conservatives defended slavery and the Dred Scott decision, others warned that political equality would give freedmen the right "to marry their daughters, and, if necessary, hug their wives." Their speeches were applauded by much of the southern press, which ridiculed the "Bones and Banjo Conventions" and the former slaves who believed themselves "competent to frame a code of laws."[2]

The first large group of elected southern Republicans, the delegates mirrored the party's social composition. About one-sixth were northerners, or "carpetbaggers" in the lexicon of their political opponents. Mostly veterans of the Union Army, many of whom had risen from private to commissioned officer during the war, carpetbaggers were the best-educated group of Republicans, numbering lawyers, physicians, and other professionals. Many had invested in cotton planting in 1865 and 1866, only to suffer heavy losses from the crop failures of those years. Talented, ambitious, and youthful (their average age was thirty-six), they now viewed politics as an alternative livelihood, and most made convention service a stepping-stone to further Reconstruction office. Carpetbaggers generally chaired the key committees and drafted the most important provisions of the new constitutions.[3]

Southern white Republicans ("scalawags" to their opponents) formed the largest group of delegates, especially in North Carolina, Georgia, Arkansas, Alabama, and Texas. Those of acknowledged standing, like Benjamin F. Saffold, son of Alabama's former chief justice, were far outnumbered by upcountry farmers, few of whom had ever held political office, and small-town merchants, artisans, and professionals, who formed no part of the established business leadership of their states. Nearly all had opposed secession, and many had served in the Union Army or been imprisoned for Unionist sentiments. Like the carpetbaggers, scalawag delegates believed the new constitutions must construct a "nobler and more enduring civilization" on the ruins of the Old South, but more immediate concerns commanded their attention, especially the proscription of Confederates and relief to debt-ridden small farmers. On racial issues, they were sharply divided. One representative of the Arkansas mountains cited Scripture and the Declaration of Independence to support his conviction that "all men are created equal," and others had worked closely with blacks in the Union League. Among Virginia's scalawag delegates were Radical leader James Hunnicutt and his political ally James Morrissey, a Richmond saloonkeeper who defeated former Governor Francis Pierpont for a seat, thanks to black support. But other scalawags, an opponent of Reconstruction remarked, "are elected with feelings opposed to the negro, however Republican they may be."[4]

Although accounting for 265 delegates, blacks were substantially underrepresented in most states (black voters proving far more willing to support white candidates than white Republicans to vote for blacks). They formed a majority of the Louisiana and South Carolina conventions, but only about 10 percent in Arkansas, North Carolina, and Texas, roughly one-fifth in Alabama, Georgia, Mississippi, and Virginia, and nearly 40 percent in Florida. In background, they mirrored already well-established patterns of black political leadership. Of those for whom biographical information is available, ninety-five had been born slaves and eighty-six free, and twenty-eight had spent all or most of their lives in the North. At least forty black delegates had served in the Union Army, and the largest occupational groups were minister (many of whom supplemented their income in other employments), artisan (mostly carpenters, shoemakers, blacksmiths, and barbers), farmer, and teacher. Only a few were field hands or common laborers. A handful of black delegates owned substantial amounts of property, but the large majority paid no state taxes (apart from poll taxes) whatever. Nearly all would go on to hold other Reconstruction offices, including 147 state legislators and 9 congressmen.[5]

These aggregate figures, however, obscure local patterns reflecting the nature of black politics and the structure of black society in different parts of the South. Nearly half of the black delegates, and a majority of those born free, served in South Carolina and Louisiana, where political organizing, led by the free urban elite, had the longest history. Indeed, in Louisiana the freeborn enjoyed a virtual monopoly of black positions, while in South Carolina they were joined by large numbers of northerners and freedmen, many of them black-belt organizers for the Union League. Georgia, with a small free population and few blacks who had served in the army or come to the state with the Freedmen's Bureau (since General William T. Sherman had refused black recruits and the Bureau had hired virtually none), saw the church provide the bulk of leadership—of the twenty-two black delegates, no fewer than seventeen were ministers. In Virginia, reflecting the greater opportunity for manumission and escape enjoyed by Upper South slaves, and the close ties between free and freed, over one-third of the slave-born delegates had gained their freedom before the war, and one delegate, a free blacksmith, had spent time in prison for assisting fugitives.[6]

The educated, articulate, and politically experienced freeborn delegates of South Carolina and Louisiana played major roles in their conventions, dominating debate and often outmaneuvering white participants. Other states produced individual leaders who took an active part in proceedings—men like William H. Grey of Arkansas, who as the free servant of Virginia Governor Henry A. Wise had attended sessions of Congress before the war; George T. Ruby of Texas, a northerner in his mid-twenties who had organized schools for the Freedmen's Bureau and risen to head the state's Union League; and fugitive slave Dr. Thomas Bayne, a veteran of Virginia black politics since 1865, and a man with "a good flow of speech, a vast amount of general knowledge, a fund of apposite and humorous anecdotes, . . . and withal a good deal of common sense."[7]

Outside Louisiana and South Carolina, however, most black delegates, lacking formal education, found "agricultural degrees and brick yard diplomas" poor preparation for the complex proceedings of a constitutional convention. They had little to say during debates, and sometimes allowed white delegates to take advantage of their inexperience. Rev. Henry M. Turner later admitted that Georgia's black delegates had been misled into believing that a poll tax to support education could not be used to limit black voting. Yet, while generally remaining silent, black delegates proved perfectly capable of judging political and constitutional questions and promoting the interests of their constituents. (In Alabama, for example, they succeeded in winning passage of an ordinance enabling black congregations to gain control of church property controlled by white trustees.) On issues of civil rights and access to education, blacks in every state formed a unified bloc, adamant that, as a Virginia delegate put it, no right "ever enjoyed by citizens prior to 1861" could now justifiably be denied them. On matters of disfranchisement and economic policy, black delegates, like white, divided, reflecting diverse social currents and political strategies within the black community.[8]

Could conventions dominated by such delegates produce constitutions attuned to the needs of the postwar South? Governor James L. Orr of South Carolina, speaking for many southern whites, thought not, pointing out, in an insulting speech to the delegates, that his state's "intelligence, refinement and wealth" were unrepresented. In fact, most of the conventions produced modern, democratic documents, "magnificent" for their "liberal principles," in the words of Jean-Charles Houzeau, editor of the New Orleans *Tribune,* the journal of New Orleans's radical free-black community. The constitutions established the South's first state-funded systems of free public education overseen by central commissioners of education, and in South Carolina and Texas made school attendance compulsory, a provision strongly supported by black delegates. State responsibilities were also expanded by clauses mandating the establishment of penitentiaries, orphan asylums, homes for the insane, and, in some cases, the provision of poor relief.

All of the constitutions guaranteed blacks civil and political rights, completing, as a Texas newspaper put it, the "equal rights revolution." They abolished holdovers from the old regime resented by blacks and whites alike: whipping as a punishment for crime, property qualifications for office and jury service, viva voce voting, and imprisonment for debt (the last termed by one scalawag a "barbarous relic of a feudal age"). Florida even granted the Seminole Indians two representatives in the state legislature. The constitutions reduced the number of capital crimes, and in three cases reorganized local government along the lines of the New England township, to overthrow local oligarchies centered in unelected county courts. South Carolina for the first time authorized the granting of divorces, and nine of the ten states recognized a married woman's separate property rights (although more to protect families against a husband's creditors than as a gesture to feminism). Antebellum bills of rights were expanded to include language from the Declaration of Independence declaring all men created equal, recognition of citizens' paramount loyalty to the federal government, and the right of blacks as well as whites to bear arms. Such provisions brought southern government into line with changes already in place elsewhere. "We want these . . . constitutions to be like our constitutions," Massachusetts Senator Henry Wilson had declared, and except for black rights (guaranteed in few northern states), they were, with many articles copied directly from the North.[9]

Embodying southern Republicans' commitment to equal rights and a New South, the conventions also revealed the party's inner divisions. Republicans seemed far abler to agree on general principles than their actual implementation—on public education but not whether schools should be racially integrated; civil and political rights for blacks but not "social equality"; the expansion of democracy but not black control of local or state governments; loyal rule but not the disfranchisement of rebels; economic modernization, but not how to balance the need for outside capital with white farmers' demands for debtor relief and blacks' desire for land. The outcome of these debates illuminated the balance of power within individual states and differing perceptions of how a stable Republican majority might be constructed.

To Conservatives, the issue of race relations offered the best means of embarrassing their foes and disrupting the Republican coalition. At every turn, they sought to place Republicans on record on such questions as interracial marriage and separate schools for black and white. Many Republicans hoped to avoid these divisive questions entirely, but opponents of Reconstruction succeeded in embroiling a number of conventions in lengthy discussions of interracial marriage. (One Georgian moved that any minister officiating at such a wedding be imprisoned for up to twenty years or deported to Liberia.) Black delegates expressed little interest in marrying white women, but some felt constrained to point out that the "purity of blood" lauded by their opponents had "already been somewhat interfered with" by planters assaulting or cohabiting with female slaves.[10]

The Conservatives were not the only delegates to raise questions of "social equality," however. A motion by Radical Richmond freedman Lewis Lindsay, ordering doorkeepers to stop segregating spectators in the convention's gallery, was narrowly defeated, with the large majority of blacks and carpetbaggers in favor, Conservatives opposed, and scalawags divided. More common was the demand for equal access to transportation and public accommodations, generally pressed by freeborn southerners or blacks from the North, many of them men of some means who, one related, had experienced "considerable discomfiture" when traveling or seeking admission to hotels and restaurants. James W. D. Bland, a free-born carpenter, raised the issue in Virginia, former New York hotel steward Tunis G. Campbell in Georgia, Ovide Gregory, the "acknowledged leader" of Mobile's free community, in Alabama, and Indiana-born army veteran Rev. James White in Arkansas. Both free and freed black delegates supported such measures, but the carpetbaggers and scalawags divided or opposed, most conventions avoided the question, neither guaranteeing equal access to public facilities nor mandating segregation. South Carolina and Mississippi enacted vague provisions barring "distinction" on the basis of color, but only Louisiana, where freeborn blacks dominated the proceedings, explicitly required equal treatment in transportation and licensed businesses. Georgia's scalawag majority, which had heard former Governor Joseph E. Brown insist that "the God of nature did not intend . . . social equality," prohibited all legislation respecting "the social status of the citizen."[11]

Even more charged was the subject of integration in education. No state actually required separate schools, an omission that led thirteen white Alabama delegates to resign from the Republican party. But only Louisiana and South Carolina explicitly forbade them. Most blacks appeared more concerned with educational opportunities for their children and employment for black teachers than with the remote prospect of racially mixed schools. Only a narrow majority of Virginia's black delegates supported Dr. Thomas Bayne's unsuccessful measure mandating such integration. Even in South Carolina, the same black delegates who praised the school integration clause as "laying the foundation of a new structure" acknowledged that both races preferred separate education. What blacks in every state rejected almost unanimously was a requirement of racial segregation. James W. Hood, later North Carolina's assistant superintendent of education, favored separate schools because nearly all white teachers, "educated as they necessarily are in this country," viewed black children as "naturally inferior." But he adamantly opposed writing segregation into the constitution: "Make this distinction in your organic law and in many places the white children will have good schools, . . . while the colored people will have none." Only the threat of integration would force states to provide blacks with "good schools" of their own.[12]

Republicans also differed among themselves over the democratization of southern politics and its political implications. With black suffrage, in most states, came legislative apportionment based either on total population or registered voters. The end of the "white basis" of representation marked the final defeat of the upcountry's long-standing battle to reduce the power of plantation counties, and led some scalawags to seek other ways of limiting blacks' statewide power. Moreover, demands by black delegates and reform-minded whites for popular election of state and local officials were countered by fears of Democratic majorities in white counties and concern among Whiggish scalawags who hoped to control local affairs in the black belt. Torn between the desire to expand popular control of government and uncertainty about the breadth of their white support, the conventions adopted contradictory policies, in some cases greatly enhancing democracy, in others, where politics triumphed over ideology, limiting it significantly.

Most democratic of all the constitutions was North Carolina's. Here, upcountry resentment at the undemocratic structure of state and local politics had a long history, the Republican party's biracial coalition appeared secure, and the convention produced what Henry Wilson termed "the most republican constitution in the land." Wilson's was an apt remark, for language evoking revolutionary-era republicanism echoed in the debates. One scalawag proposed to abolish the state senate, the home of "special advantage and protection of a particular class of citizens." Another denounced the state's property qualifications for office and its antiquated system of legislative representation as deriving from "the old fallacy that the people are incapable of self-government." Although the senate survived, the delegates replaced the old state Executive Council and county courts appointed by the General Assembly with state and local officials chosen by popular vote, and made judges from the supreme court down to justices of the peace elective.[13]

At the other end of the political spectrum stood Georgia and Florida, whose conventions, dominated by moderate scalawags, adopted ingenious methods of making Reconstruction palatable to white voters and minimizing what Georgia's first Republican governor called "the danger of negro suffrage." Georgia's county-based system of legislative apportionment restricted the influence of the geographically-concentrated black population, and the governor or the General Assembly were empowered to appoint virtually every official above the level of justice of the peace—a reversal of the state's prewar practice. The constitution also omitted any mention of blacks' right to hold office, and required that jurors be "worthy and intelligent" citizens, giving local officials ample authority to exclude blacks. Florida's convention, controlled after a series of complex maneuvers by a coalition of business-oriented white Republicans and Whiggish Conservatives, likewise skewed legislative representation in favor of white counties, gave the governor "imperial" powers of appointment, and authorized the legislature to establish an educational qualification for voting. Designed to attract white voters to a moderate Republican party devoted to Florida's economic development, the constitution, commented the *Nation*, "surpasses in conservatism that of any State in the Union."[14]

Another issue pitting commitment to democracy against party survival was the disfranchisement of former Confederates. Many Republicans could not reconcile their party's democratic rhetoric with proposals to strip large numbers of "rebels" of the franchise. Others, like Virginia's Hunnicutt, found themselves agreeing with the Conservative definition of voting as a conventional right that society could restrict for its own protection. Although upcountry scalawags, especially those who had suffered for their Unionist beliefs or who came from areas devastated by the South's internal civil war, supported disfranchisement most vehemently, the issue followed no simple pattern, for it became embroiled in Republican factionalism and divergent perceptions of the party's prospects of attracting white voters.[15]

Five states disfranchised few or no Confederates—Georgia, Florida, and Texas, where moderates committed to luring white Conservatives into the party controlled the proceedings; South Carolina, with its overwhelming black voting majority; and North Carolina, where the party's white base seemed secure. (North Carolina's mountain delegates, however, objected to their constitution's leniency.) At the behest of upcountry scalawags and some Radical carpetbaggers, Alabama and Arkansas barred from voting men disqualified from office under the Fourteenth Amendment as well as those who had "violated the rules of civilized warfare" during the Civil War, and required all voters to take an oath acknowledging black civil and political equality. Even this was not enough for one delegate from the strife-torn Arkansas upcountry, who "would have disfranchised every one of them. I have suffered too much at their hands." Louisiana, where the likelihood of white support appeared bleak, disfranchised a long list of Confederates, from newspaper editors and ministers who had advocated disunion to those who had voted for the secession ordinance, but exempted men willing to swear to an oath favoring Radical Reconstruction. Mississippi and Virginia, to the chagrin of Whiggish Republicans, also barred considerable numbers of "rebels" from voting.[16]

A hallmark of upcountry Republicanism, disfranchisement evinced less interest among black delegates, many of whom seemed uncomfortable with a policy that appeared to undermine the party's commitment to universal suffrage and might set a precedent for future limitations on black voting. "I have no desire to take away the rights of the white man," declared former slave Thomas Lee, an Alabama delegate. "All I want is equal rights in the court house and equal rights when I go to vote." Others feared the policy might embarrass the party nationally. Virginia black delegate James W. Bland inquired urgently of Congressman Elihu Washburne, "Is it policy to further disfranchise *Rebels?* . . . Give me your advice immediately." Many blacks, however, recalling the conduct of ex-Confederate officials during Presidential Reconstruction and Conservative delegates' refusal to accept the legitimacy of black political rights, were determined that such men must not regain political hegemony. In general, black voting on the issue paralleled that of the white Republican leadership, favoring leniency in Georgia and North Carolina, and—with the exception of James W. Bland and a few others—following Hunnicutt in supporting proscription in Virginia. Louisiana's black majority found itself divided by the issue. The New Orleans *Tribune* had long opposed disfranchisement, arguing, "If we refuse the franchise to any class, it can as well be withheld from us," and some black delegates repudiated the clause barring many ex-Confederates from voting. Yet a northern reporter found black delegates more proscriptive than their white counterparts, and a solid majority, including all four identified as former slaves, voted in favor of the provision.[17]

On economic matters, the developmental spirit prevailed. Union League president Allston Mygatt told Mississippi's delegates that with a modern constitution "large land estates shall melt away into small divisions, . . . mechanism [would] flourish, agriculture become scientific, internal improvements be pushed on." The desire to promote economic growth led Alabama's convention to establish a Bureau of Industrial Resources, and Georgia's to move the state capital from the sleepy village of Milledgeville to the thriving commercial entrepôt of Atlanta (where, Joseph Brown explained, "the State can build a splendid granite Capitol, hewn out of the Stone Mountain, with convict labor, at a very light cost"). The new constitutions allowed extensive public aid to railroads and other ventures, although sometimes adding safeguards against abuse. (Mississippi and Virginia barred the loan of state credit to corporations, and Texas prohibited railroad land grants, but all three allowed direct financial subsidies.) Alabama's delegates, who resented the aid the state's railroads had given the Confederacy, petitioned Congress to construct a national system of cheap transportation to counteract the "monopoly principle" and high railroad freight rates. But North Carolina's, not content to wait for legislative action, voted two million dollars in immediate railroad aid. Several states authorized the granting of charters under general incorporation laws, and some for the first time established limited liability for corporate stockholders. Many voided usury laws entirely, or dramatically increased the legal ceiling on interest rates.[18]

The desire to attract capital and reassure bondholders and prospective investors doomed the Radicals' demand for an "*ab initio*" Reconstruction that would wipe away existing state debts and all laws, including corporate charters and railroad land grants, dating from the Confederacy. In every state, carpetbaggers were the strongest proponents of economic modernization, with upcountry scalawags and blacks, especially former slaves, more cautious. An attempt by Alabama Radical Daniel Bingham to levy a fifty-thousand-dollar tax on railroads receiving state aid won the support of upcountry white Republicans and a majority of blacks, but was defeated by a coalition of carpetbaggers, Conservatives, and black-belt scalawags. North Carolina's carpetbaggers joined with blacks and Conservatives to validate prewar state bonds, held in large quantities by railroad companies, but an attempt to establish a commissioner of immigration fell before the opposition of Conservatives, scalawags, and blacks. (One black delegate chided those hoping to use state funds to assist immigrants—"if anything was to be distributed, the poor black should have it.") Georgia, as usual, had the most cautious black delegates, whose unanimous opposition helped carpetbaggers and urban scalawags defeat a clause, supported by many upcountry Republicans, authorizing the legislature to repeal or modify corporate charters. And in South Carolina, free blacks from the North, some already involved in railroad ventures, others hoping to share in the impending state largesse, opposed limiting aid to internal improvements. "This is a progressive age," declared Pennsylvania-born Jonathan J. Wright, and the government should be left free "to do those things for the public good which the public good requires."[19]

Even more complex were the debates and alignments surrounding debtor relief, an issue that had won Republicans considerable support in the North Carolina, Georgia, and Alabama upcountry. Facing the loss of their land, many indebted small farmers viewed the relief question in stark class terms. "This is a strife between capital and labor," declared a Georgia scalawag delegate, "between the wealthy aristocrats and the great mass of the people." Actually, "wealthy aristocrats" were among those clamoring for relief. "The whole South is now bankrupt," a planter's wife lamented, and throughout the region estates were being advertised for sale to liquidate debts. One Alabama plantation, valued at three hundred thousand dollars in 1860, was sold at public auction and the family evicted.[20]

Whatever their political differences, upcountry farmers and black-belt planters shared a common interest in retaining control of their land. Others viewed debtor relief with less enthusiasm. Merchants forced to meet the demands of out-of-state suppliers would be ruined if local clients could avoid repaying advances. Economic promoters feared northerners would never loan capital to railroads and other enterprises if barred from taking recalcitrant debtors to court. And many blacks agreed with the Georgian who told his former owner, "The freedmen cannot be benefitted by this measure. They owe no debts." Blacks, moreover, knew that Presidential Reconstruction stay laws had often enabled employers to avoid obligations to their laborers, and had no desire to help rescue the planter class from liquidation. Staying the collection of debts, James W. Hood told North Carolina's convention, would benefit "those who now hold lands" and "prevent the poor people from ever getting land." James Hunnicutt held the same view, and, alone among the new constitutions, Virginia's prohibited stay laws entirely.[21]

Only in Georgia, which abrogated all debts dating from before 1865, did a substantial number of black delegates support stay measures, subordinating their constituents' desire for land to the attempt to woo white voters. In Mississippi a majority of black delegates, as an alternative to debtor relief, urged the army to establish a public works program for the destitute of both races (a project in which military authorities displayed little interest). In South Carolina, freeborn Charleston tailor Robert G. DeLarge and northerner William J. Whipper urged delegates to heed "the voice of the impoverished people of the state." But Francis Cardozo opposed any step that might prevent the breakup of "the infernal plantation system." By a narrow margin, the delegates called upon the army to suspend the collection of debts; scalawags overwhelmingly favored the measure, with blacks, free and slave, strongly opposed.[22]

In preference to stay ordinances, which benefited rich and poor debtors indiscriminately, blacks generally favored the homestead exemption, a more selective form of relief. Measures shielding a certain amount of real and personal property from seizure by creditors guaranteed that an indebted small farmer or artisan would not lose his land, tools, or household furniture. "The petitions of the $20,000-men have been heard by Andrew Johnson," declared an interracial group of Virginia Republicans, calling upon their convention to secure the homes of "the $1,000 or $500-men" against foreclosure. Every constitution except Louisiana's incorporated a homestead exemption—ranging from fifteen hundred dollars worth of property in North and South Carolina to five thousand in Arkansas and Texas—while barring its use against laborers' claims for wages, and, in some cases, tax liabilities. With southern land values having fallen sharply since the war, the larger exemptions effectively protected the vast majority of white southerners. "There are not many men," one correspondent remarked, "whose farms and residences . . . would bring $5000 in cash were they sold tomorrow." Blacks generally favored low exemptions, hoping to benefit small farmers while compelling those with "fifty or eight thousand acres" to part with some of their land.[23]

If debtor relief temporarily stabilized southern landholding patterns, tax reform seemed to offer an opportunity to reshape southern class relations. At Virginia's Radical-dominated convention, delegates black and white expressed bitter resentment against the antebellum tax system and the inordinately high state and local poll taxes of Presidential Reconstruction. "The poor people have to bear all the burdens of taxation in this State," declared black delegate Thomas Bayne, noting that freedmen paid poll taxes of three to four dollars while "vacant lots worth thousands of dollars were taxed but fifty cents." James Hunnicutt pointed out that low land taxes encouraged planters and speculators to accumulate large uncultivated tracts, which a heavy land tax might force onto the market. "If we do not tax the land," declared Frank Moss, a black delegate who described himself as "a working man," we might just as well not have come here to make a Constitution. . . . I would rather pay a high tax upon land and work it myself than to work for other people for nothing."[24]

Some blacks proposed to make the tax structure progressive, through an extra levy on uncultivated land or, as one Louisiana delegate suggested, exempting farms of less than sixty acres from taxation altogether. The only such measure adopted, however, was one in Virginia authorizing a special tax on annual incomes of over six hundred dollars. Generally, the new constitutions rested state revenues on a property levy, a principle already well established in the North, but a striking departure in southern fiscal policy. All property—land, personal possessions, stocks and bonds—would henceforth be taxed equally according to its true monetary value, drastically increasing the burdens of landowners from planter to small farmer while benefiting commercial interests, artisans, and professionals previously burdened by license fees, and, of course, propertyless freedmen. Despite upcountry opposition, the constitutions also authorized modest poll taxes, with the revenue earmarked for the new school systems. Blacks generally supported these imposts, fearing that public education financed entirely by property taxes would quickly lose white support.[25]

When the constitutional conventions assembled, many Conservatives, in the words of a New Orleans newspaper, feared a policy of "unadulterated agrarianism" (the nineteenth century's term for attacks on private property). With "Negroes and Tories" in control, a Georgian warned, "a general division of lands" was likely, followed by "laws regulating the price of labor and the rent of lands—all to benefit the negro and the poor." In one form or another, the interrelated questions of land and labor came before a majority of the conventions, but the results hardly lived up to the hopes or fears kindled in 1867. In the face of free-labor principles and northern Republicans' anticonfiscation sentiments, Radicals failed to find an effective means of enhancing the bargaining power of black labor or promoting the goal of land distribution. Politics and ideology combined to frustrate the economic aspirations that had animated grass-roots black political organizing in 1867.

Several conventions awarded mechanics and laborers liens for wages on the property of their employers, and Texas prohibited the importation of "coolies" and the establishment of "any system of peonage," but free-labor assumptions doomed other attempts to intervene on behalf of black workers. An attempt by South Carolina Confederate Army deserter James M. Allen to regulate rents, setting one-half of the crop as a maximum, failed, as did a Virginia carpetbagger's proposal to establish an eight-hour day for "hired labor." (This prompted a committee report declaring legislation on the subject unwise: "the number of hours to be devoted to labor is a matter of contract.") Louisiana's constitution included a provision, strongly supported by carpetbaggers and Conservatives, barring the legislature from "fixing the price of manual labor." Wealthy Creole employers like sugar planters Pierre G. Deslonde and Auguste Donato favored the prohibition, as did prominent New Orleans free blacks to whom any interference in the labor market recalled the hated contract regulations of General Nathaniel P. Banks. Other New Orleans delegates, however, including some free blacks, opposed the provision, hoping to satisfy the eight-hour demands of the city's labor movement, as did the few ex-slaves voting, probably hoping for future state regulations favoring the laborer.[26]

Both black and white Radicals spoke of the need to provide freedmen with land and encourage the breakup of the plantation system. "I have gone through the country," reported Richard H. Cain in South Carolina's constitutional convention, "and on every side I was besieged with questions: How are we to get homesteads?" A few constitutions took modest steps toward meeting this demand. Texas offered free homesteads to settlers on the state's vast public domain, and Mississippi provided that land seized by the state to satisfy tax claims must be sold in tracts of not greater than 160 acres. Louisiana set an even lower limit of fifty acres, but defeated a proposal to limit the amount any individual could purchase at such sales. New Orleans free blacks favored the first clause but unanimously opposed the second, possibly hoping to acquire sizable holdings themselves. Most aggressive was South Carolina's convention, which au-

41

thorized the legislature to establish a state commission to purchase land for resale on long-term credit. Soon after the convention opened, the delegates killed a motion by black carpetbagger Landon S. Langley, a veteran of the famous 54th Massachusetts, that confiscation and disfranchisement be "forever abandoned." Sixty percent of white Republicans favored Langley's proposal, but a large majority of both southern free blacks and freedmen opposed it, the most significant black support coming from northerners like Langley, carriers of free-labor ideas. But confiscation never came to the floor, partly because the delegates feared Congress would reject a constitution it deemed too radical.[27]

With each state producing its own mixture of radical and moderate elements, the new constitutions failed to satisfy black economic aspirations, but introduced changes in the southern political structure that appeared dangerously radical to those who preferred the ways of the Old South and Presidential Reconstruction. Democrat and Whig alike, the bulk of the region's traditional leadership now mobilized in opposition.

As for the Republicans, the conventions revealed the sources of ideological unity within the party, but also underscored the diversity of political interests and strategies, and the debilitating factionalism, that would plague southern Republicanism throughout its brief career. Nonetheless, optimism reigned among southern Republicans, both black and white. The dawn of a New South seemed truly to be at hand. "There is a sense of security displayed by our people," Louisiana black leader P. B. S. Pinchback had warned in 1867, "that is really alarming. They seem to think that . . . the Great Battle has been fought and the victory won." More realistic was the judgment of Governor William Brownlow, a veteran of the turbulent political wars of Tennessee: "Never was such a conflict witnessed as we are to have."[28]

Notes

1. David Macrae, *The Americans at Home* (New York, 1952), 138; Malcolm C. McMillan, *Constitutional Development in Alabama, 1798–1901* (Chapel Hill, 1955), 114–17; Ernest L. Bogart and Charles M. Thompson, *The Industrial State, 1870–1893* (Springfield, 1920), 3; William M. Jenkins to James L. Orr, January 31, 1868, South Carolina Governor's Papers, South Carolina Archives; Peter J. Rachleff, *Black Labor in the South: Richmond, Virginia, 1865–1890* (Philadelphia, 1984), 45–48; Schuyler Colfax to John C. Underwood, January 7, 1868, Elihu B. Washburne to Underwood, December 7, 1867, John C. Underwood Papers, Library of Congress; *National Anti-Slavery Standard,* January 4, 1868.

2. Autobiography of George Teamoh, manuscript in Carter G. Woodson Pa-

pers, Library of Congress; *Debates and Proceedings of the Convention Which Assembled at Little Rock* . . . (Little Rock, 1868), 88–89, 431, 637; Cal M. Logue, "Racist Reporting During Reconstruction," *Journal of Black Studies* 9 (March 1979): 335–50.

3. Richard L. Hume, "Carpetbaggers in the Reconstruction South: A Group Portrait of Outside Whites in the 'Black and Tan' Constitutional Convention," *Journal of American History* 64 (September 1977): 313–30; *Congressional Globe,* 41 Congress, 1 Session, 431; Jack B. Scroggs, "Carpetbagger Constitutional Reform in the South Atlantic States, 1867–1868," *Journal of Southern History* 27 (November 1961): 475–77.

4. Richard L. Hume, "Scalawags and the Beginnings of Congressional Reconstruction in the South" (Paper delivered at the American Historical Association annual meeting, 1978); McMillan, *Alabama,* 121; Raleigh *Daily Standard,* February 24, 1868; *Arkansas Convention Debates,* 661–62; Richard G. Lowe, ed., "Virginia's Reconstruction Convention: General Schofield Rates the Delegates," *Virginia Magazine of History and Biography* 90 (July 1972): 347, 352; M. J. Keith to Henry Watson, Jr., October 2, 1867, Henry Watson, Jr., Papers, Duke University.

5. Richard L. Hume, "Negro Delegates to the State Constitutional Conventions of 1867–69," in Howard Rabinowitz, ed., *Southern Black Leaders of the Reconstruction Era* (Urbana, 1982), 129–53; 42 Congress, 2 Session, House Report 22 (Ku Klux Klan Hearings), South Carolina, 1241–44. I wish to thank Professor Hume for making his list of delegates available to me. My own list, compiled from his data as well as manuscript sources and recent studies of southern black politics during Reconstruction, differs slightly from his. As can best be determined, the number of black delegates by state was as follows: Alabama 17, Arkansas 8, Florida 19, Georgia 36, Louisiana 50, Mississippi 16, North Carolina 14, South Carolina 71, Texas 10, and Virginia 24.

6. Ted Tunnell, *Crucible of Reconstruction: War, Radicalism and Race in Louisiana, 1862–1877* (Baton Rouge, 1984), 231–33; Thomas Holt, *Black Over White: Negro Political Leadership in South Carolina During Reconstruction* (Urbana, 1977), appendix; Edmund L. Drago, *Black Politicians and Reconstruction in Georgia* (Baton Rouge, 1982), 37–39; Lowe, "Virginia Convention," 348–60.

7. Joseph M. St. Hilaire, "The Negro Delegates in the Arkansas Constitutional Convention of 1868: A Group Portrait," *Arkansas Historical Quarterly* 33 (Spring 1974): 43, 61; Carl H. Moneyhon, "George T. Ruby and the Politics of Expediency in Texas," in Rabinowitz, *Southern Black Leaders,* 363–68; New York *Times,* January 11, 1868.

8. George Teamoh Autobiography, in Woodson Papers; Ku Klux Klan Hearings, Georgia, 1041; *Alabama Session Laws,* 1868, 176–77; *The Debates and Proceedings of the Constitutional Convention of the State of Virginia* (Richmond, 1868), 197.

9. *Proceedings of the Constitutional Convention of South Carolina,* 2 vols. (Charleston, 1868), 47–50; Jean-Charles Houzeau, *My Passage at the New*

Orleans Tribune: A Memoir of the Civil War Era, ed. David C. Rankin, trans. Gerald F. Denault (Baton Rouge, 1984), 143; William P. Vaughan, *Schools for All: The Blacks and Public Education in the South, 1865–1877* (Lexington, 1974), 50–52; John P. Carrier, "A Political History of Texas During the Reconstruction, 1865–1874" (Unpub. diss., Vanderbilt University, 1971), 326; *The Campaign Speech of Hon. Foster Blodgett . . .* (Atlanta, 1870), 6; Suzanne Lebsock, "Radical Reconstruction and the Property Rights of Southern Women," *Journal of Southern History*, 43 (May 1977): 201–7; Nelson M. Blake, *The Road to Reno: A History of Divorce in the United States* (New York, 1962), 63, 234; *Congressional Globe*, 40 Congress, 1 Session, 144. The texts of the Reconstruction constitutions may be found in Francis N. Thorpe, ed., *The Federal and State Constitutions*, 7 vols. (Washington, 1909).

10. *Journal of the Proceedings of the Constitutional Convention of the People of Georgia* (Augusta, 1868), 143; *Arkansas Convention Debates*, 363, 491–99, 501; Paul C. Palmer, "Miscegenation as an Issue in the Arkansas Constitutional Convention of 1868," *Arkansas Historical Quarterly* 24 (Summer 1965): 99–119.

11. *Journal of the Constitutional Convention of the State of Virginia* (Richmond, 1867 [1868]), 147–52; *The Debates and Proceedings of the Constitutional Convention of the State of Virginia* (Richmond, 1868), 154; Drago, *Black Politicians*, 40–41; *Journal of the Proceedings of the Convention of the State of Alabama* (Montgomery, 1868), 15; St. Hilaire, "Arkansas," 64; Joseph H. Parks, *Joseph E. Brown of Georgia* (Baton Rouge, 1977), 398.

12. McMillan, *Alabama*, 152; *Virginia Convention Journal*, 333–40; *South Carolina Convention Proceedings*, II, 889–901; Raleigh *Daily Standard*, March 7, 1868.

13. *Congressional Globe*, 40 Congress, 2 Session, 2691; "Resolution of Mr. Congleton, February 14, 1868," Secretary of State Papers, Constitutional Convention, North Carolina Archives; Raleigh *Daily Standard*, February 14, 1868.

14. Scroggs, "Carpetbagger Constitutional Reform," 485–88; Rufus B. Bullock, "Reconstruction in Georgia, 1865–70," *The Independent* 55 (March 1903): 672; Drago, *Black Politicians*, 40–44; New York *Times*, February 5, 1868; Richard L. Hume, "Membership of the Florida Constitutional Convention of 1868: A Case Study of Republican Factionalism in the Reconstruction South," *Florida Historical Quarterly* 51 (July 1972): 5–7, 15–16; Samuel Walker to Elihu B. Washburne, June 12, 1868, Elihu B. Washburne Papers, Library of Congress; *Nation*, May 21, 1868.

15. *Arkansas Convention Debates*, 658; *Virginia Convention Debates*, 528–33; Carrier, "Texas," 301, 313–14.

16. *Alabama Convention Proceedings*, 30–34; *Arkansas Convention Debates*, 320–21, 673; William A. Russ, Jr., "Disfranchisement in Louisiana (1862–1870)," *Louisiana Historical Quarterly* 18 (July 1935): 575–76; Hamilton J. Eckenrode, *The Political History of Virginia During the Reconstruction* (Baltimore, 1904), 98–102; *Journal of the Proceedings in the Constitutional Convention of the State of Mississippi* (Jackson, 1871), 732.

Eric Foner

17. McMillan, *Alabama,* 129; James W. D. Bland to Elihu B. Washburne, March 15, 1868, Washburne Papers; *Georgia Convention Proceedings,* 299–300; *Journal of the Constitutional Convention of the State of North Carolina* (Raleigh, 1868), 251; *Virginia Convention Journal,* 221, 239–40, 271, 283–84, 295; New Orleans *Tribune,* November 25, 1866; *Official Journal of the Proceedings of the Convention for Framing a Constitution for the State of Louisiana* (New Orleans, 1868), 183, 259; New York *Times,* February 1, 1868.

18. *Mississippi Convention Proceedings,* 4; Atlanta *Daily New Era,* March 11, 1868; Mark W. Summers, *Railroads, Reconstruction, and the Gospel of Prosperity: Aid Under the Radical Republicans, 1865–1877* (Princeton, 1984), 25; *Congressional Globe,* 40 Congress, 2 Session, 808; *Arkansas Convention Debates,* 62–64; Jonathan Wiener, *Social Origins of the New South, 1860–1885* (Baton Rouge, 1978), 148–51.

19. Summers, *Railroads,* 23; *Alabama Convention Proceedings,* 137; *North Carolina Convention Journal,* 204, 214, 310; Leonard Bernstein, "The Participation of Negro Delegates in the Constitutional Convention of 1868 in North Carolina," *Journal of Negro History* 34 (October 1949): 408; *Georgia Convention Proceedings,* 336–37; *South Carolina Convention Proceedings,* I, 249–50, II, 659–62.

20. Atlanta *Daily New Era,* February 2, 1868; Mrs. W. A. Kincaid to Mrs. E. K. Anderson, August 20, 1867, Kincaid-Anderson Papers, South Caroliniana Library; Robert A. Gilmour, "The Other Emancipation: Studies in the Society and Economy of Alabama Whites During Reconstruction" (Unpub. diss., Johns Hopkins University, 1972), 123–26.

21. Jerrell H. Shofner, "A Merchant Planter in the Reconstruction South," *Agricultural History* 46 (April 1972): 291–96; A. Stevens to Benjamin Conley, January 30, 1868, Benjamin Conley Papers, Atlanta Historical Society; A. W. Spies to Charles Jenkins, November 30, 1866, Georgia Governor's Papers, University of Georgia; Joshua Hill to John Sherman, January 10, 1868, John Sherman Papers, Library of Congress; *Annual Cyclopedia,* 1866, p. 13; Raleigh *Daily Standard,* February 3, March 6, 1868; Richmond *New Nation,* quoted in Raleigh *Daily Standard,* January 17, 1868.

22. *Georgia Convention Proceedings,* 198–99, 252, 458–59; William C. Harris, *The Day of the Carpetbagger: Republican Reconstruction in Mississippi* (Baton Rouge, 1979), 134–35; *South Carolina Convention Proceedings,* I, 108–14, 125–30, 148.

23. *Virginia Convention Debates,* 87–88; J. H. Thomas, "Homestead and Exemption Laws," 1–17, 137–50; New York *Times,* February 5, 1868; *Georgia Convention Proceedings,* 385; *South Carolina Convention Proceedings,* I, 137, 141.

24. *Virginia Convention Debates,* 487, 652, 686–87, 695, 713–15, 722.

25. *Virginia Convention Debates,* 104; J. Mills Thornton III, "Fiscal Policy and the Failure of Radical Reconstruction in the Lower South," in J. Morgan Kousser and James M. McPherson, eds., *Region, Race, and Reconstruction: Essays in Honor of C. Vann Woodward* (New York, 1982), 349–94; *Virginia Convention Journal,* 129–30, 138.

26. New Orleans *Picayune*, February 20, 1868; Alan Conway, *The Reconstruction of Georgia* (Minneapolis, 1966), 148; *South Carolina Convention Proceedings*, I, 194; *Virginia Convention Journal*, 297; *Louisiana Convention Journal*, 26, 120–21.

27. *South Carolina Convention Proceedings*, I, 380; *Journal of the Reconstruction Convention, Which Met at Austin, Texas*, 2 vols. (Austin, 1870), I, 895; *Mississippi Convention Proceedings*, 739; *Louisiana Convention Journal*, 266–67, 1465; *South Carolina Convention Proceedings*, I, 43; Springfield *Weekly Republican*, December 21, 1867.

28. James Haskins, *Pinckney Benton Stewart Pinchback* (New York, 1973), 52; William G. Brownlow to ?, May 8, 1867, copy in Loring Moody Papers, Boston Public Library.

"Social Equality," Miscegenation, Labor, and Power

Nell Irvin Painter

One need not agree with the whole work of U. B. Phillips to see that Americans—southern and otherwise—have long been fascinated by the racism that he called the central theme of southern history. Race means many things to Americans, but so long as it continues to flourish as a way for Americans to define one another it will cast its spell. In this essay about racism, sex, and power I will start with an insight of my colleague Joel Williamson, who observes that "ultimately, there is no race problem in the South, or in America, that we, both black and white, do not make in our minds."[1] The mind problems—values, mores, ideologies—are precisely what characterize societies and provide the subject matter that anthropologists, sociologists, and some historians study, seeking to delineate the ways in which people arrange themselves within their worlds. Williamson rightly accords mentalities a good deal of attention, as I will, examining black as well as white views of miscegenation and white supremacy. Taking a cue from Williamson, I will discuss rhetoric as well as events, subjective as well as objective realities, noting the many silences in the dialogues that occurred between whites and whites, blacks and blacks, and blacks and whites.

While respecting the importance of the subjectivities surrounding race, I will also stress what I see as the fundamental point of racism, the economic and political domination of the poorest part of the southern working class. Money and laws express mentalities, but they also create material conditions that are far more solid.

In the American South the seizure, maintenance, and cession of power

47

have long been expressed in racial terms, as though race were a real, not a social category whose fundamental function has been to rank people and keep them in place. As Edmund Morgan has shown, it is no accident that racism hardened as masses of southern workers were sealed into hereditary servitude.[2] After the late seventeenth century, individuals of a variety of shades of skin color and textures of hair—some physically indistinguishable from "whites"—were called Negroes, whose main identity was that of an enslaved working class. Out of the infinite variety of human physiognomy the makers of southern laws created two categories, two "races." This scheme—which simplified empirical realities considerably—benefited the majority by oppressing the minority and outlived slavery by more than a century. An early twentieth-century white supremacist, Myrta Lockett Avary, summed up the enduring relationship between racial identity and economic function: "The white man does not need the negro as *litterateur,* statesman, ornament to society. . . . What he needs is agricultural labour."[3]

The men and incidents that I use to embody white supremacy date from the turn of the twentieth century: Josephus Daniels and the North Carolina white-supremacy campaign of 1898, the writings of Thomas Dixon, and the Atlanta race riot of 1906. If this era did not necessarily produce more racial violence, it assuredly did circulate an enormous amount of rhetorically violent propaganda.[4] White-supremacist rhetoric had existed during the antebellum period, but the addition of politics into the mixture came with black enfranchisement in the 1860s. Enfranchisement made poor men into voters and undermined—or seemed to undermine—the politics of deference that planters dominated. In terms of issues and style, large numbers of black voters shook the political plum tree during Reconstruction by voting and influencing public policy in the interests of the poor, thereby creating pressures for disfranchisement.[5]

White-supremacy campaigns, speaking of race, not class, were aimed at taking the black masses out of politics and realigning politics along lines that political elites considered favorable. By stressing race, white supremacists reinterpreted the opposition against the lower-class masses (which black men represented in subjective and objective realities) as political actors. In the 1870s men like General Martin Gary of South Carolina spoke lines that became commonplace later on. Democratic power in the South seemed to require black disfranchisement, which in turn demanded an extraordinary mobilization of the white electorate. Democrats had discovered in the early 1870s that ordinary political campaigns failed to bring large numbers of white voters to the polls, never mind into the streets armed.

Sex was the whip that white supremacists used to reinforce white solidarity, probably the only whip that would cut deeply enough to keep poor whites in line. Political slogans that spoke straightforwardly of property or wealth (which not all whites held) had failed to rally whites en masse. However, nearly all white men could claim to hold a certain sort of property, in wives, sisters, and daughters. When women were reduced to things, they became property that all white men could own. The sexually charged rhetoric of "social equality" invited all white men to protect their property in women and share in the maintenance of all sorts of power (including the economic and political, which disproportionately benefited the better-off) in the name of protecting the sexuality of white womanhood.

The most emotional issue of southern race relations that grew out of slavery was sex. Orlando Patterson points out that in the antebellum South, as in every other slave society, masters claimed the right to have sex with their female slaves (and probably slave boys as well).[6] Sex was a kind of human property that slavery transferred involuntarily from slaves to masters. Like labor, it was a stolen thing.

But in the American South, the theft of sex occurred in a society dominated by evangelical Protestantism. As personal morality had become more important with the growth of the Baptist, Methodist, and Scotch-Irish Presbyterian churches, extramarital sex had become identified with sin in a more tortured way than in more formalist religion. By the late eighteenth century what Lillian Smith summed up as the "race-sex-sin spiral" in which "guilt, shame, fear, lust spiralled each other" already existed.[7] This association of sex and race spiced with sin endured into the turn of the twentieth century, when white supremacists put it to political purposes. The resulting argument was rickety at best, but few examined it closely at the time. In fact, the combination was so piquant that Thomas Dixon's version enjoyed popularity as a novel, *The Clansman* (1905); a play, *The Clansman* (1906–7); and as a film, *Birth of a Nation* (1915), that continues to be shown. In successful lecture tours of the whole United States, Benjamin "Pitchfork" Tillman of South Carolina replayed the same themes.

Identifying the figure of the white woman with civilization, Josephus Daniels, Tom Watson, Benjamin Tillman, and Thomas Dixon drew on dualities established before the Civil War. The slave South, like all other slave societies, cloistered women of the master class, elevating the mistress/virgin and simultaneously debasing the slave/whore. Drawing on these conventions at the turn of the twentieth century, white supremacists predicted that the ultimate outcome of black voting would be what they called "social equality" or race mixing, which would entail the downfall of civilization. White supremacists did not carefully define what they meant by civilization, but they assigned to themselves the favorite qualities of chauvinists throughout the Western world. Whether they are sexists, racists, anti-Semites, or pornographers, chauvinists divide the world into two, assigning to women/blacks/Jews the sphere associated with nature: savagery, emotions, lack of control, sexuality. The stereotypical notions that incited mob violence in the South—the bleeding female victim and the black beast rapist—united two aspects of otherness, blacks and women, through sex. No other conjunction could seem so seriously to threaten civilization. This emphasis on the sexuality of women who belonged to men and the division of mankind into two utterly dissimilar parts are characteristics of what Susan Griffin has called the pornographic mind. I will return to this concept later in this essay.

While white-supremacist rhetoric never let the fear of women as a force of nature percolate up to the conscious level, the obsessive concern over white women's sexuality hints at an identification with disorder. (White) women's sexuality, exploited by black men, could ruin "the South."

Seeking in the late 1890s to overthrow the biracial fusionist regime in North Carolina, Josephus Daniels heated up the rhetoric of disfranchisers, joined sex and race, and warned that black voting endangered "the sanctity of [white] women."[8] The virulent white-supremacist campaign culminated in the downfall of the fusionists and the death of eleven black men in what came to be known as the Wilmington riot.

In Georgia would-be disfranchisers like former Populist Tom Watson studied the North Carolina model and embellished the same line: "[The Negro] grows more bumptious on the street. More impudent in his dealings with white men; and then, when he cannot achieve social equality as he wishes, with the instinct of the barbarian to destroy what he cannot attain to, he lies in wait . . . and assaults the fair young girlhood of the south. . . . It is time for those who know the perils of the negro problem to stand together with deep resolve that political power shall never give the negro encouragement in his foul dreams of a mixture of races."[9]

In Atlanta in the summer of 1906 the overt themes of sex, race, and politics resonated with fears other than the political. An evangelist had recently awakened familiar American fears (indeed, Western fears) of what strong drink might do to the lower class—in the South identified as blacks—while temperance agitation reinforced apprehensions stirred by the performance of the play *The Clansman,* which made much of the figure of the black-beast-rapist. Finally, the summer witnessed continual agitation in the newspapers about rapes of white women by black men.

Extra editions announcing rape after rape within a matter of hours set off a white mob that attacked the roughest and the most refined black sections of the city. By the time the Atlanta riot ended, some twenty-five blacks and one white had died, and the white supremacists had won the election. In both Wilmington and Atlanta the three provocative concepts of sex, race, and political power combined with a potency that is difficult to imagine today.

The issue of crime (defined primarily as black on white rape) appears repeatedly in white-supremacist writing, but without assumptions that figure in discussions of criminality today: that poor people commit most of what our society defines as crimes; that crime rates increase during economic hard times; and that sentences vary according to the class and race of both victim and offender (that is, white offenders from the better-off classes are punished less harshly, and defendants whose victims are whites are punished more harshly than defendants convicted of assaulting blacks). Feminists stress further that rapists and wife-beaters come from all classes and races.

When it comes to actual crimes—real rapes—at the turn of the twentieth century, the record is full of silences. There seems not to have been any investigation into the alleged crime wave in eastern North Carolina at the end of the nineteenth century, even though supposed black crime furnished the rationale for a bloody attack on blacks in Wilmington and for subsequent black disfranchisement. In Atlanta in 1906 Ray Stannard Baker found no attempt to discern the number of actual rapes. He investigated the twelve rapes and attempted rapes that black men were said to have committed before the riot. He found two rapes, three attempts, and all the other attacks imaginary or unfounded. Baker also discovered three rapes of white women by white men, which had attracted little or no attention in the newspapers, even though one assault was especially grisly. Baker either did not think to check rapes of black women by black or white men or such crimes were not in police records. Whichever was the case, Baker did not mention black women as victims in his discussion of rape in Atlanta.[10]

Many at the turn of the century defined rape as a crime whose only victims were white women.[11] Every reason in the world exists to suspect that a great deal of crime, including what we call rape (sexual intercourse with a woman of any class or race against her will through the use or threat of force), existed in turn-of-the-century Atlanta, perhaps also in Wilmington and surrounding rural eastern North Carolina, for the city of Wilmington was probably not an exception to the southern rule of inadequate police forces. Southern society seems generally to have been poorly served by law enforcement, and observers noted with horror the ferocity of black criminals and the blood lust of white mobs, but not as though they were manifestations of the same angry culture.[12] Well into the twentieth century, native southerners like Lillian Smith, Richard Wright, and Maya Angelou spoke of the fear pervasive in the region.[13] In 1898 the United States was just emerging from a long and deep depression, which was accompanied by a crime wave in the South.

In 1906 Atlanta was a fast-growing city that had an unusually high crime rate, even in comparison with cities with larger total populations and larger black populations. The city struck Ray Stannard Baker as ill-policed, and he noted that the mob freely looted stores, whether owned by blacks or whites, in the pursuit of black victims. Under such conditions, one would expect a good deal of crime of all sorts, but whether this would have been interracial crime is another matter.

Homicide in the nineteenth- and twentieth-century South, and rape in the twentieth century, followed similar patterns. Most murders involved a black assailant and a black victim. Less frequent were murders involving white assailants and white victims, then white assailants and black victims, then, rarely, black assailants and white victims. I have been unable to find any statistics on rape in the nineteenth or early twentieth century, but according to mid-twentieth-century statistics, far and away the most common rape cases brought to trial involved black assailants and black victims, then white assailants and white victims. In much smaller numbers were rape cases with black assailants and white victims and rare instances of trials of white assailants and black victims.[14] In short, if actual crimes of violence had been occurring with increased frequency in Wilmington or Atlanta at the turn of the twentieth century, the largest number would most likely have involved black attackers and black victims, then white attackers and white victims.

The anger that incited the mob in Atlanta was not connected to actual crimes, and no indictments or convictions of alleged rapists followed the riot. According to the businessmen's committee of inquiry, none of the victims was a "vagrant," the class from which rapists reputedly came. Instead the riot victims were reported as "honest, industrious and law-abiding citizens and useful members of society," though modest members of the working class.[15] Attacking blacks indiscriminately, the mob seems to have been completely indifferent to the identity of actual rapists.

On the black side of the color line the specific question of black rape of white women met silence. Two black journalists, Alex Manley, who was in the midst of events in Wilmington, and Ida B. Wells, tried to explain black-on-white rape away or to show that it was not the main cause of lynching. After the riot in Atlanta, northern black newspapers blamed the riot on the rhetoric of the political campaign—which most likely did, in fact, incite the violence—circumventing the charge of rape and making no attempt to disprove the white-supremacist accusation that black men raped white women. I suspect that black journalists (educated, middle-class people susceptible to class prejudice against the poor) secretly feared that the black lower classes might actually be capable of such attacks.

Reading evidence backwards is a risky matter, and I hesitate to conclude that because an Eldridge Cleaver in the 1960s said he took revenge on white men by raping white women—having practiced up, he said, on black women—that black men of similar mentality existed in the nineteenth or early twentieth centuries. It is certain, however, that if more than a tiny handful of black men of Cleaver's viciousness had acted they would have turned up in the historical record and in folklore. Instead, no evidence of either sort exists to show that black men were especially prone to raping white women. More to the point, those leveling the charge undermined their credibility by their unconcern about actual guilt—their willingness to murder suspects and suspects' relatives or associates on flimsy evidence. Wells found that although rape supposedly explained lynching, only about one-third of 728 black lynch victims in the late nineteenth century had even been charged with rape. Using 1903 figures, Baker found that only 21 of 104 lynch victims had been suspected of rape or attempted rape.[16]

Today it is not possible to discover how many and what sort of rapes occurred, because what really happened seemed relatively unimportant at the time. There simply is no good evidence to show much of anything about actual occurrences of rape, only that it was a matter of high emotional salience. Rape was a symbol related to other symbols of southern society, one of which was "social equality."

"Social equality" meant people of two races, usually including black men, sitting down together at table or on a train, sharing a smoke at a club, or belonging to the same organization on a footing of equality. When a servant sat with an employer, that was not "social equality." "Social equality" meant associating as equals, which, according to the logic inherent in the slogan, would lead inexorably to black men's marrying white women. Josephus Daniels led a howling campaign against President Theodore Roosevelt's "insult" to the South, which was the president's sharing a meal at the White House with Booker T. Washington. Yet no one, not even Daniels, cited a case when a black dinner guest walked off with a daughter of the host on his arm.

"Social equality" existed only in the negative. Yet it was so potent a symbol that whites and blacks of all persuasions united in insisting that they opposed it. To be for "social equality" was to favor race mixing, which no one could support. Denouncing "social equality" was as necessary for southern whites as denouncing communism became in the 1950s (and for similar social and political reasons). As in red-baiting, the burden of proof fell on the accused, so that no one pressed Josephus Daniels to present his proof. In an atmosphere that white supremacists had charged with racism simple neutrality would not suffice, at least not in public. Not to deplore "social equality" and race mixing was tantamount to confessing to a lack of race pride. On both sides of the color line, race pride was the equal of patriotism in time of war and anticommunism in cold war.

The rhetoric of "social equality" was couched in racial terms, but its deeper meaning was packed with class distinctions rooted in slavery. Slavery had made races into classes, with black people as the South's basic and symbolic labor force. Class consciousness was not nearly so acute as race consciousness, in rhetoric, at least. Many southern whites worked and were poor, of course, but the concepts of race in the antebellum South contained the inherent assumption that whites = planters, blacks = slaves.

Although the word *class* rarely appeared in turn-of-the-century writing about the South, the hierarchy of racism expressed a clear ranking of classes, in which the word *white,* unless modified, indicated a member of the upper class and *black,* unless modified, equalled impoverished worker. So deeply embedded in racial categories were assumptions about class that deviation from these assumptions required the use of adjectives: *poor* white, *middle-class* black.

Southern slaves were overwhelmingly agricultural workers, and from them their masters expected not only labor but also the deference associated with the rural working class in areas shaped by British custom: hats off before masters, avoidance of looking masters in the eye, humility manifested as uncertainty. White supremacists were exceedingly touchy about infractions of this code of employer-employee patterned deference, and contempt in employees, often called "impudence," was occasionally a capital offense in the postwar South. "Impudence" threatened the employer-employee aspect of race relations and seemed to hint that the employee (actual or symbolic) was independent of the employer (actual or symbolic).

What racism did in the South after the Civil War was further to embed class relations into the etiquette of race relations. Blacks, all blacks, were supposed to act like servants with all whites. Segregation codified the

54

relationship between people of the better class, which was one racial group (whites), and people of the lower class, which was another racial group (blacks). One reason southern whites opposed "social equality" was that it seemed ludicrous to them on what they did not recognize as class grounds. Here a fantasy will help make the point.

In the 1870s Charles Manigault, a Charleston aristocrat, was looking back on the events of 1865 and philosophizing about the future. First he wrote about blacks, then he intended to speak about whites, who did not keep his attention, so he drifted back to blacks. Manigault said he pitied blacks, whose hopes for freedom were so misguided that they believed that they would become the social equals of whites. By "whites" Manigault meant people like himself, very rich planters whom the war had left their long years of formal education, gentlemanly status, and considerable real property. Manigault imagined that blacks would spin as elaborate a daydream of social equality as he himself did, in which " 'Cuffy' (the Beau of Ebony Belles) will be seen *Dancing with the Governors Daughter,* when Old Mauma 'Sucky,' so highly esteemed by her Coler'd Brethren for the fine *pan-cakes* she made, will in *their opinion,* not only be received in the best society, but courted & flattered, by distinguished *White Gentlemen.*"[17]

The mismatch of classes makes Manigault's fantasy absurd: a gardener dancing with debutantes, gentlemen courting a cook. This horror of the mixing of the classes was an unacknowledged aspect of "social equality," and it was rooted in the unremunerated labor that masters extorted from slaves as well as in the masters' sensitivity to gradations in the social hierarchy.

Thomas Dixon's stories of the Ku Klux Klan were flagrantly racist, and as in most American writing about race, he confounded race and class. The most important people in his work were whites, all of whom functioned as aristocrats. Dixon's *The Clansman* (unlike some of Thomas Nelson Page's work) did not include poor white villains, so that in Dixon all whites display the attributes of power, not only wealth and education (formal or informal), but also height, slenderness, and refinement.[18] These are the natural rulers of Dixon's made-up society, in which whites unfitted for leadership do not exist.

Below whites/aristocrats in Dixon's scheme are mulattoes, middling people, middling in refinement, middling in beauty, middling in intelligence. They are interested in attaining the accouterments of whiteness—political influence and white mates—but they are not prepared to use anything more forceful than cunning. Dixon associates his mulattoes closely with sex, and it is they who introduce the issue of "social equal-ity," particularly the Silas Lynch character in *The Clansman,* who pro-poses to a young white woman.

The linking of mulattoes and sexuality occurs in other contemporary southern white writing.[19] Myrta Avary thought of mulatto women as in-herently impure, mostly because she assumed that they were the products of immediate race mixing. She overlooked the possibility that light-skinned blacks could be the descendants of light-skinned blacks. For Avary, conse-quently, only black black women might be morally honest (that is, engage in sex only in marriage); race mixers and the products of race mixing could not be.[20] Walter Hines Page, who lived in New York and was as moderate a white southerner as could be imagined, fell into similar habits of thought. His autobiographical novel *The Southerner* (1901) includes a scene in which the protagonist is seduced by a young woman of mixed blood.

Writers like Alfred Holt Stone, a Mississippi planter widely considered an expert on race relations in the early twentieth century, weighed the pur-ported qualities of black men of mixed blood and pure blood, to the disad-vantage of mixed bloods, whose "white blood" supposedly made them ambitious; men of pure "black blood" were more patient and respectful toward whites. Stone's "mixed blood" example was W. E. B. Du Bois, the picture of impatience, and his paragon of blackness (although in reality a brown, not a black man) was Booker T. Washington.[21] Most white writers tried to avoid this sort of discussion because it contained contradictions that were hard to avoid. Whites who deplored race mixing ran into the fact that blacks who displayed qualities that Americans prized—education, wealth—were more likely than not of mixed blood. Generally any discus-sion of mulattoes by whites homed in on sexuality.

No matter how much blacks and whites denounced "social equality," the actual existence of a body of people in the South of obviously mixed race put many in a quandary. For the most part, whites tended not to bring up the obvious unless pressed, but prominent blacks flung the facts in their faces repeatedly. Whenever someone like Benjamin Tillman began a tirade defending lynching as the punishment for the unspeakable crime, a black person in the audience or in the columns of a newspaper would remind him that white men, not black, were the South's premier race mixers.

Self-appointed spokesmen for "the South" would then concede that in the antebellum days a few masters might have dallied in the slave quarters, but that the whites who mixed races, in general, were the "vicious," that is, they belonged to the lower class. Here the handy conventions of white su-premacy (white = upper class, black = lower class) served well, for by por-traying white miscegenators as the poor and the criminal, white supremacists read them out of the white race entirely. White race mixers, by this logic, were not *real* whites. They could not be, because (real) whites possessed an inherent passion for racial purity.

If, in a system that classified anyone of African descent, however attenuated, as black, whites could fairly easily sweep under the rug the actual race mixing that occurred between white men and black women, blacks could not. Yellows and browns were as much Negroes as blacks, so Negroes had to tussle with matters of miscegenation.

An egalitarian consensus among blacks that grew out of the denial of racist tenets shaped the discussion—or lack of it—of different shades of color among blacks. Whereas most whites believed that one's worth depended on one's "blood," one's physical inheritance, which was unalterable or not very susceptible to change through manipulations such as education and increased income, blacks usually traced individual attainment to favorable circumstances. Blacks denied that race predicted one's abilities, insisting that given the proper advantages, any man—black, brown, or yellow—could become a gentleman, any woman a lady. If some blacks prospered and others suffered, the difference was not to be sought in the "blood." Taunting white supremacists, however, blacks unfailingly yielded to temptation and pointed out that "the best blood of the South" flowed in the veins of Negroes and that white aristocrats, not white lowlife, had fathered the South's mixed bloods. Even so, blacks would not concede that the descendants of planters were superior to the descendants of slaves on both sides.

The refusal to link achievement with color is remarkably consistent in black nonfiction writing, in which every black person is the potential equal of the other, from Mrs. Booker T. Washington to the mother of the poorest and least-educated sharecropping family in Mississippi. Blacks censored themselves in nonfiction, which almost never includes mention of intraracial distinctions of complexion.

In black fiction, in contrast, the quandaries abound. How to deal with the obvious fact that most of the leaders of the race—the wealthy, the educated, the published—were men and women of mixed blood? How to face the fact that blacks as well as whites equated light complexions with Negro feminine beauty? How to explain that brown and yellow people often discriminated against black people socially, as though the latter belonged to a lower class? Like Americans generally, blacks who wrote on such themes described individual attributes rather than the advantages or injuries of class. And, like other Americans, black fiction writers produced characters in which relative whiteness/yellowness symbolized refinement and blackness symbolized coarseness. Charles Chesnutt followed these un-

57

spoken rules, so that his Reena Walden character in *The House Behind the Cedars* (1900), so fair that she can pass for white, speaks standard English and is naturally refined even before attending school. Yet Chesnutt's characters include in *The Marrow of Tradition* (1901) a crude, poor white politician and an uneducated but astute black black man, as though to demonstrate that virtue does not invariably accord with color.

Still, black fiction writers often accepted the conventions of white supremacy unconsciously, and the confusion of values remained in black fiction at the turn of the century; for the most part yellows stood for the Negro elite in a way parallel to the white supremacists' appropriation of aristocracy for the white race. But there was an articulate exception. A black novelist from Memphis, Sutton Griggs, wrote creatively about mixed and pure blood. His solution was to balance his characters carefully by sex and shade. His yellow men marry black women, his black men marry yellow women, and all of them are genteel. Griggs's future Negro race would finally emerge a uniform, medium brown. Like most other black writers of the late nineteenth and early twentieth centuries, Griggs created characters, especially women, of relentless refinement.

One minor character in the white-supremacist mythology never appears in black fiction: the dissolute black woman, on whom white supremacists placed the blame (with low white men) for miscegenation. Most whites—and some blacks—agreed that black women's morals were so deplorable that they welcomed the advances of white men. This stereotype of black women was rooted in slavery and in class status after slavery. As Susan Brownmiller points out, women of subject or conquered populations and women who belong to groups susceptible to abuse, such as European Jews and American blacks, have long been considered especially seductive by men of more powerful groups.[22] That particular groups of women have been seen as outside the moral system of others has long provided men an excuse for rape. During the last two millennia, men have turned the vulnerability to sexual assault of groups of women into a reputation for sensuality.

As slaves and as members of a despised racial minority, black women belonged to categories labeled "libertine." As working women, too, they were vulnerable to the abuses of employers and fellow workers and likely also to be misunderstood by people of the better-off classes. Kathy Peiss notes that at the turn of the century working-class culture in the North horrified middle-class social workers with its sexual explicitness, free use of liquor, and moral flexibility.[23] It should come as no surprise that in the South black women (most of whom worked in agriculture or as domestic servants) were said by white supremacists to have no morals. By extension, there could be no such thing as the rape of a black woman.

While whites saw black women's sexual availability as an inherent trait, blacks either denied it or ascribed it to conditions: poverty, lack of education, the corrupting influence of slavery. Blacks emphasized further black women's long-standing powerlessness before white men. "Oh, if there is any one thing under the wide canopy of heaven horrible enough to stir a man's soul, and to make his very blood boil," wrote William Craft in his slave narrative, "it is the thought of his dear wife, his unprotected sister, or his young and virtuous daughters, struggling to save themselves from falling a prey to such demons!"[24]

This anger, prevalent in the writing of black men, interprets attacks on the bodies of black women as an insult to black men, as though the mistreatment of women served as a proxy in a struggle between black and white men. This view echoes an approach to women as old as the Bible and seemingly common in the South: that women are the property of men and that raping a woman is an attack on the man who owns her. Black men, like white men, were not immune to this interpretation of relations between the sexes.

Black women's writings, like the narratives of white women who had been in Indian captivity, betray little of this anger over sexual exploitation, as Frances Foster demonstrates. Female autobiographers such as Harriet Jacobs (Linda Brent) and Elizabeth Keckley mention sexual abuse, but as briefly and obscurely as possible. They see themselves as powerless victims whose loss of virtue was not their own fault. In this their approach resembles that of black male narrators. But more important, female narrators do not stress their identity as victims, as male narrators do.

Women seem to wish to suppress unfortunate occurrences in order to demonstrate that they succeeded in transcending oppression to achieve something praiseworthy, which they interpret also as a service to their race. Female narrators had not initiated sexual relations with white men and were not indifferent to sexual exploitation, but they do not define themselves in terms of sexual victimization. These women, showing that even the humblest American could become autonomous and contribute to her society, chose not to emphasize the aspect of their experience that involved rape, the ultimate victimization, the extreme proof of powerlessness.

Black women's reticence about sexual victimization was not unique. With the noteworthy exceptions of Rebecca Latimer Felton, a fiery white supremacist and leading purveyor of the black-beast-rapist line, and Myrta Lockett Avary, white women also did not dwell on their sexual vulnerability. Nor were they publicly apprehensive about the threat of "social equality" or the possible existence of marauding black men. Southern white women's main public issue at the turn of the century was temperance, and, later, suffrage.

In the most famous "rape" case of the twentieth century, the Scottsboro case, the two alleged victims seem to have been intimidated into claiming that they had been assaulted by the young black men, and one of the women recanted later and joined the Scottsboro defense. In that same decade, a group of white southern women, led by Jessie Daniel Ames, worked to halt the practice of lynching, claiming that it was an insult to white women. As Jacquelyn Hall explains, the Association of Southern Women for the Prevention of Lynching realized that lynching terrorized white women as well as blacks, furthering the goals of both sexual and racial control.[25] Whether the women victims of rape were black or white, they were far less bent on publicity and revenge than their men. The struggle over "social equality," race mixing, and violence was fundamentally economic and political, thereby an affair of men.

This is not to say that the panoply of laws and traditions designed to immobilize and weaken blacks as workers and to humiliate them as individuals did not apply to women. It most certainly did. But with women disfranchised and with men as the usual heads of household and therefore as the main political and economic persons in their families, the emotional nexus of power connected black and white men; black women's victimization was virtually incidental to white supremacy. White supremacists intended black women to remain vulnerable as workers and available as sex objects, but the main targets of violent, collective, emotionally charged racism at the turn of the century were men, poor black men, the foundation of the southern working class. Educated and well-to-do black men also fell victim to racism, of course, as in the politically charged burning to death of a black postmaster in South Carolina in 1898. But as in the case of black women, the victimization of prosperous black men, who were few in number, was almost incidental to the immobilization of millions of black workers.

The regime of racial oppression set in place at the turn of the century had several aspects that are perhaps familiar, but let me underline how multifaceted the controls were. Vagrancy laws pressured all blacks to remain employed (though hard times created black as well as white tramps throughout the region). Convictions for petty crimes that poor people were likely to commit, such as selling cotton after dark or stealing livestock, led to the chain gang, and convicts were likely to be leased to planters or industrialists. Contracts that ran for twelve months kept workers from switching jobs in pursuit of better wages. Crop lien laws tied agricultural workers to their employers or suppliers through debt and bound them into the cash-crop economy. Tenancy laws lodged control of shared crops in the hands of landowners, from seeding to marketing, so that sharecroppers were in practice wage workers rather than joint proprietors of a crop.[26]

On top of controls on laborers' mobility and freedom to change employers laid down in law, black workers faced other difficulties as employees. Night-riding and other forms of violence made planters into protectors, providing further means of dominating workers, whose lack of education kept them too uninformed and too lacking in self-assurance to challenge planters' authority. Low wages made saving next to impossible while hard work increased the attraction of liquor and other ways of spending what little was on hand. Finally, the southern tradition of deference that was both racist and paternalist made it dangerous for employees to dispute their employers' words. All this together meant that mobility, except downward, was extraordinary.

Poor whites were also subject to the debilitating economic effect of this "Prussian road" toward development. They, like blacks, became increasingly enmeshed in the web of farm labor, as the proportion of tenants and sharecroppers of both races increased in the South. But given the racism of the society as well as everyday class oppression masquerading as racial hierarchy, poor blacks found themselves at a greater economic disadvantage than poor whites. Through laws and racist traditions, well-off whites were able to increase their economic power at the cost of poor blacks and poor whites, but the harder hit were the blacks, particularly rural laborers.

Disfranchisement also increased the political power of well-off whites vis-à-vis the poor, black and white. The radical decline in ballots cast by poor men meant that officeholding reverted to the well-to-do, who furthered their own ends. Even legislators elected by the Farmers' Alliances in the late 1880s, who had as candidates measured up to the "Alliance yardstick," failed to perform in office in ways that would help modest farmers—for instance, by passing any version of the subtreasury plan. Perhaps large numbers of southern farmers would have lost their land or never have been able to afford to buy without the narrowing of the franchise. But clearly legislatures dominated by the better-off did little to ease the plight of the poor and everything to assure employers ample supplies of docile labor at low wages. Summing up labor relations in the late nineteenth-century South, Pete Daniel sees the law as the central point of compulsion.[27]

Tenancy and disfranchisement crippled all the poor in the South, but

61

they affected black southerners more harshly than white. Poll taxes and secret ballots disfranchised many poor whites, but Democratic politicos continued to appeal to them at election time, and their voting was not likely to be resisted with nearly the same vigor as blacks'. Poor whites benefited from the money wages and relative mobility of textile employment. In cities like Birmingham, moreover, white workers held jobs classified differently from "Negro jobs," the latter being harder, dirtier, and less remunerative. Even though blacks and whites might be doing the same tasks, the highest-paid blacks would make about the same as the lowest-paid whites.

Poor whites thought they had something to lose by being treated equally with blacks, because they *did* have something to lose—political standing and wages, not to mention other little perquisites of whiteness such as knowing there is someone who is considered your inferior. The shibboleth of "social equality" worked at the bottom, even though working-class whites profited less from white-skin privileges than the wealthy. Poor whites who banded together with rich whites against blacks were not simply victims of a false consciousness, at least not in the short run. They may have been members of the working class, but they were still better off than most blacks.

White supremacists of various stations fashioned a series of controls over blacks that exceeded the economic and political, which I have just listed. This third category of race relations has often been summed up as segregation, but I will borrow a term from Susan Griffin and call it the "pornographic" aspect of racism. Griffin describes what she calls the "pornographic mind," which is the same as the "chauvinist mind," and which, objectifying what it hates—whether women, blacks, or Jews—seeks to injure and humiliate the object. She links pornography to sadism, stressing the pornographer's obsession with rituals of hurting and humiliating.[28] Chauvinists like Adolph Hitler and Thomas Dixon both played out the fantasy of the dark man raping the fair woman, but for Hitler the man must be a Jew; for Dixon, a black. And for both the proper response was violence that punishes everyone within the symbolic category of the other. Whether on the mundane or catastrophic level, the essence of pornographic power was degradation.

The system of segregation was an obvious display of pornographic power, relegating blacks to inferior public services and treating them all like servants (for example, making any black person enter buildings through the back or service door, refusing any black person the titles Mr., Mrs., Miss, and calling any black person by a first name). The formula of "separate but equal," like "social equality," was never meant to materialize. In a white-supremacist society, "separate but equal" was nonsensical, for segregation was intended to insult blacks and to remind them at every turn of their lower status. Segregation was the everyday aspect of racial degradation that corresponded to symbolic class roles for the races.

Just as the effective end of black political power in the late nineteenth century did not reassure white politicians who continued to fear—or at least say they feared—the possibility of "Negro domination," so segregation and other humiliations did not sufficiently reassure white supremacists of their pornographic power. It was not by chance that they seized on the cry of "rape" to incite violence that was often blind, for the very word resonates with the pornographic symbols of degradation and sexuality. Here the real or imagined violation of a woman served as a pretext for another kind of rape.

Rapes of a sort did occur when Ku Klux Klansmen administered beatings, white supremacists of North Carolina and Georgia incited riots, and nameless whites joined lynch mobs. But these lynchings, symbolic rapes, were by white men against black men. Symbolic rapes, like actual rape against women, were rituals of power and degradation, as white men burned, whipped, and murdered in an attempt to close the circle of their power over black men. Aping the forms of legal executions, these symbolic rapes constituted the bodily aspect of the maintenance of white men's physical power over black men.

Viewed in an anthropological light, the rituals of riots and lynchings may be interpreted as reaffirmations of community values. But the values in question upheld the oppression of the poorest people in the society and today appear obscene. White-supremacist riots and lynchings were rituals whose analogues are more nearly fraternity gang-bangs than rites of passage. Racial violence, so much out of place in a democracy priding itself on the rule of law, was simply another aspect of the maintenance of a multifaceted power that had enormous class import but that was expressed in racial terms. There was, of course, oppression that was racial, for the oppression of a race of people was the obvious point of segregation and other forms of racial humiliation, from the virulent to the niggling. But the larger, deeper meaning of white supremacy was the creation and maintenance of a powerless working class that was as vulnerable to the whim of employers as possible and as unfitted as could be for competition with working-class whites.

It is true that the need for pornographic power existed only in the "mind" of southern society, or, more to the point, in the "mind" of a portion of the South. It is also probably true that the exercise of pornographic power indicates that the symbolic rapists of black men felt insufficiently powerful. But what must also be remembered is something that the Association of Southern Women for the Prevention of Lynching knew in the 1930s: that lynching was the product of white supremacy and that the very notion that one group ought to hold power over another was at fault. More than that, the need for pornographic power reinforced and was reinforced by the realities of other kinds of domination, economic and political.

Not until 1940 could the Association of Southern Women for the Prevention of Lynching proclaim the passage of the first year without a lynching, which means that the practice continued for a very long time.[29] What ended the regular exercise of pornographic power was not the assurance that blacks had been sufficiently intimidated to stay in their place. It was rather that blacks migrated out of areas where lynchings and riots occurred and employers lost their work force. Riots ruined the business climate of cities in which they took place, so that white employers and businessmen came to discourage racial violence out of sheer business sense.

More fundamentally, the undermining of white supremacy nationally brought change. Blacks gained moral and political standing in American society, and black power, attenuated as it was in the early twentieth century, challenged white supremacy bit by bit, in organizations such as the Niagara Movement, the Negro Business League, and the National Association for the Advancement of Colored People. It is not by chance that the worst of white supremacist mouthings ended between 1915 and 1925, for these were the years when blacks began to make themselves felt as workers, political actors, and intellectuals in the North. An articulate handful of individuals (most noticed in Harlem) demonstrated that blacks were also writers and social scientists. Their white allies—social workers, publishers, and anthropologists—also publicized facts that challenged white supremacy. By the second quarter of this century, Congress was considering antilynching legislation and several southern states had passed statutes that opposed the practice in name, at least. White supremacy's loss of legitimacy was largely the result of a struggle that went back to Frederick Douglass and William Lloyd Garrison and extended right through the twentieth century.[30] Without this campaign against the notion that racial domination is legitimate, the exercise of pornographic power—like the exercise of other kinds of power—would have continued as an acceptable means of maintaining the southern version of the right of the privileged to exploit the poor.

Nell Irvin Painter

Notes

I would like to acknowledge the support of the Russell Sage Foundation, Nellie McKay, Mary Kelley, George Shulman, Orlando Patterson, and the New School CSSC and CHS "Think, Then Drink" Seminar.

1. Joel Williamson, *The Crucible of Race: Black-White Relations in the American South Since Emancipation* (New York, 1984), 522.
2. Edmund S. Morgan, *American Slavery, American Freedom: The Ordeal of Colonial Virginia* (New York, 1975), 295–337.
3. Myrta Lockett Avary, *Dixie After the War: An Exposition of Social Conditions Existing in the South, During the Twelve Years Succeeding the Fall of Richmond* (New York, 1906), 394.
4. I do not mean to say, however, that racial violence and white supremacy were more acute at the turn of the twentieth century than at any other time following the institution of slavery in the South. Slavery itself was a brutal system, resting on violence and threats of violence, but there is no way of counting up how many men and women were beaten and how many women were raped in slavery. It is also not possible to know how many blacks were the victims of rioters and lynchers before the Chicago *Inter-Ocean,* National Association for the Advancement of Colored People, and Tuskegee Institute began keeping lynching statistics in the late nineteenth and early twentieth centuries. My reading of congressional testimony indicates that the level of bloodshed was exceedingly high in the 1860s and 1870s. Lacking evidence to draw any but the most general conclusions about violence against blacks before the 1880s, I use turn-of-the-century rhetoric and violence as examples because the evidence is close at hand. I do see racial violence declining after the First World War, however, for reasons I explain at the end of the essay.
5. In the 1850s Republicans in Louisiana exempted items of subsistence (bacon, corn) from debt seizure. In South Carolina in 1876 the knowledge that his constituency was poor agricultural workers prevented the Republican governor from sending troops to force striking rice workers back to work. In neighboring Georgia, the Democratic governor felt no such pressure, as black Republican voters no longer played a prominent part in the politics of that state.
   I should add here that although blacks have suffered the most extreme disfranchisement, other blocs and coalitions of voters seeking to express the interests of the poor also have not lasted in this country. In the late nineteenth century, neither the Farmers' Alliances, Knights of Labor, or People's Party was able to translate class-based issues into durable political gains. Like other groups who expressed themselves politically as working people, the masses of black southerners lost their voice in politics.
6. Orlando Patterson, *Slavery and Social Death: A Comparative Study* (Cambridge, Mass., 1982), 261.
7. Lillian Smith, *Killers of the Dream,* rev. ed. (New York, 1961), 121.

65

8. Josephus Daniels, *Editor in Politics* (Chapel Hill, 1941), 302.

9. Quoted in C. Vann Woodward, *Tom Watson, Agrarian Rebel* (New York, 1963 [1938]), 379.

10. Ray Stannard Baker, *Following the Color Line* (New York, 1964 [1908]), 5.

11. One interesting exception occurred in Murray County, Georgia, in 1893, when a band of eighty white men broke into jail and freed a white man convicted of raping a white woman. See Edward L. Ayers, *Vengeance and Justice: Crime and Punishment in the Nineteenth-Century American South* (New York, 1984), 259.

12. For example, see Baker, *Following the Color Line,* 180, 186–87. It is difficult to draw a line between riots and lynching beyond the following two distinctions: riots occurred in urban areas, lynching mostly in the countryside; and rioters rarely claimed that their many victims were the actual perpetrators of the supposed crimes that had touched off the riots in the first place. Lynchings had one or rarely two victims who were alleged to be connected to specific criminal acts, real or imagined. Otherwise my generalizations here about riots also apply to lynchings, which were aspects of the same phenomenon.

13. Lillian Smith, *Strange Fruit* (New York, 1944) and *Killers of the Dream,* rev. ed. (New York, 1961), 92, 144; Walter White, *The Fire in the Flint* (New York, 1924) and *Flight* (New York, 1926); Richard Wright, *Black Boy: A Record of Childhood and Youth* (New York, 1945), 30–33 passim; *Uncle Tom's Children* (New York, 1938); and interviews with Katherine Du Pre Lumpkin and Maya Angelou.

14. Ayers, *Vengeance and Justice,* 231, and Susan Brownmiller, *Against Our Will: Men, Women and Rape* (New York, 1975), 216.

15. Baker, *Following the Color Line,* 15.

16. Ida B. Wells (Barnett), *On Lynchings: Southern Horrors, A Red Record, Mob Rule in New Orleans* (New York, 1969 [1895]), 14; Baker, *Following the Color Line,* 199.

17. Charles Manigault Memoranda, Manigault Papers, Southern Historical Collection, University of North Carolina at Chapel Hill (emphasis and erratic capitalization in the original).

18. Unwittingly Dixon (and other white supremacists and Anglo-Saxonists of the turn of the twentieth century) were tapping into stereotypes that had been circulating since antebellum times and had done service against the Irish in the North. See Dale T. Knobel, *Paddy and the Republic: Ethnicity and Nationality in Antebellum America* (Middletown, Conn., 1986), 32 and illustrations following 156.

19. Abolitionists also associated sexuality with women of mixed race, notably the famous fugitive Ellen Craft. See R. J. M. Blackett, *Beating Against the Barriers: Biographical Essays in Nineteenth-Century Afro-American History* (Baton Rouge, La., 1986), 98.

20. Avary, *Dixie After the War,* 397–98.

21. Alfred Holt Stone, *Studies in the American Race Problem* (New York, 1908), 431–35.

22 Brownmiller, *Against Our Will*, 22–23, 124, chapters 3 and 4.

23. Kathy Peiss, " 'Charity Girls' and City Pleasures: Historical Notes on Working-Class Sexuality, 1880–1920," in *Powers of Desire: The Politics of Sexuality*, ed. Ann Snitow, Christine Stansell, and Sharon Thompson (New York, 1983), 77, 83.

24. Quoted in Frances Foster, " 'In Respect to Females . . .': Differences in the Portrayals of Women by Male and Female Narrators," *Black Literature Forum* 15 (Summer 1982): 67. Although the vulnerability of slave women to sexual assault from masters is a common source of resentment in slave narratives, William Craft, married to a woman who looked white and who therefore reminded British and American whites of the sexual abuse in slavery, had a personal motive for stressing this evil. See also Fanny Kemble's similar remarks regarding slave masters' abuse of slave women in Brownmiller, *Against Our Will*, 166.

25. Jacquelyn Dowd Hall, " 'The Mind That Burns in Each Body': Women, Rape, and Racial Violence," in *Powers of Desire*, ed. Snitow, Stansell, and Thompson, 339, and *Revolt Against Chivalry: Jessie Daniel Ames and the Women's Campaign Against Lynching* (New York, 1979), 153, 194–96.

26. See Pete Daniel, "The Metamorphosis of Slavery, 1865–1900," *Journal of American History* 66 (June 1979); Harold D. Woodman, "Postbellum Social Change and Its Effect on Marketing the South's Cotton Crop," *Agricultural History* 56 (January 1982): 215–30; and "Sequel to Slavery: The New History Views the Postbellum South," *Journal of Southern History* 43 (November 1977): 523–54.

27. Pete Daniel, "The Metamorphosis of Slavery," 95.

28. Susan Griffin, *Pornography and Silence: Culture's Revenge Against Nature* (New York, 1981), 2, 15, 22, 46–47, 79.

29. Although lynchings no longer occur with late nineteenth- and early twentieth-century frequency, the practice has not ended, as events in Mobile, Alabama, in 1981 and Howard Beach, New York City, in 1986 indicate.

30. In the 1930s and 1940s the German Nazi movement and the Holocaust also served greatly to undermine the respectability of racism.

The South and South Africa: Political Foundations of White Supremacy

George M. Fredrickson

In the early 1980s three major studies appeared, two by historians and one by a sociologist, making detailed comparisons of historical developments in South Africa and the American South, or a representative part of it. The three were my *White Supremacy*, John Cell's *The Highest Stage of White Supremacy*, and Stanley Greenberg's *Race and State in Capitalist Development*.[1] The authors were not aware of each other's work in the formative stages of their respective enterprises, and no dialogue or cross-fertilization took place among them prior to publication. This essay is an attempt to deal with some of the issues raised by two of the books—Cell's and Greenberg's—from the vantage point of the third.

All three studies paid considerable attention to the political aspect of white supremacy, to the role of the state in establishing and maintaining racial dominance. Both Cell and Greenberg were centrally concerned with understanding and explaining the efforts in the South and South Africa during the modern capitalist era to use government and law for purposes of racial discrimination. I devoted much of my study to probing the long-term development of the attitudes, ideologies, and practices that led up to the mature politics of racial domination, but made it clear that what Cell termed "the highest stage of white supremacy" had not been reached until the full force of the modern state was put behind a caste system of race relations. I could have said more about the political foundations and implications of white supremacy during the period which has preoccupied my comparativist colleagues—that is, roughly from the late

68

nineteenth century to the 1960s. By doing so now, I can apply my mode of interpretation to some new problems and also build on the insights of Cell and Greenberg to develop a clearer understanding of the later and "higher" stages of white supremacy.

Clearly, as both Cell and Greenberg demonstrate, there was a major intensification and extension of state action designed to buttress white privilege in the southern states beginning around 1890 and in South Africa after the end of the Anglo-Boer War in 1902. In the South, this was the era of legalized "Jim Crow" and disfranchisement; in South Africa, it saw the implementation of the kinds of policies originally called "native segregation" that were later extended, elaborated, and systematized as the modern structure of domination known as apartheid. In both instances, the intensification of legalized discrimination occurred at a time of economic modernization or, to be more specific, capitalist development. According to conventional modernization theory, the kind of societal changes associated with industrialization, urbanization, and technological advancement are supposed to erode status differences based on "ascription" and replace them with those based on "achievement."[2] But in these cases the reverse occurred. Racial ascription was emphasized and enforced more strongly than ever, despite "modernization" in other areas. This obvious fact has led historians and social scientists to reconsider the relationship between capitalist industrialization and racial discrimination. One of two possibilities would seem to remain: either preindustrial patterns of racial hierarchy were so deeply entrenched in the cultures of these traditionally white-supremacist societies that they forced the new order arising from industrialization to adapt to them, rather than vice versa, or there was a positive affinity between capitalist development, in some of its stages at least, and discriminatory action against lower caste groups.[3] Both propositions are plausible and can be supported with evidence from the southern and South African cases. But is it really necessary, as some scholars seem to think, to choose between them? Inherited racial attitudes and the interests of "class actors" during capitalist development can also be viewed as independent variables that in some circumstances reinforce each other to create new and more extreme forms of oppression and under other conditions work at cross-purposes.

In the case of the South, we have more than an example of how a "modern" racial order was imposed; we can also see how one was overthrown. Does the demise of legalized segregation in the southern states during the 1960s provide any kind of model or precedent for the future of apartheid in South Africa? This question of burning contemporary interest might be illuminated by a comparative analysis of the origins and character of the

69

two systems of state-enforced segregation and discrimination that arose almost simultaneously on opposite sides of the globe.

Antecedent to the rise of Jim Crow in the South was the destruction of a racial order based on slavery by the Civil War and Reconstruction. Viewed as a system of racial domination, slavery did of course involve the state. Slaveholders felt that their security and well-being depended on control over local, state, and federal governments. Their loss of control, or even substantial influence, over the federal government precipitated secession from the Union. Although slaveowners needed a friendly state that would come to their aid in time of slave insurrections, slaves were governed to a very limited degree by public authorities. The masters themselves provided day-to-day governance and "law enforcement" to such an extent that descriptions of the plantation as a mini-state are only a slight exaggeration.[4] Emancipation not only destroyed a labor system; it also undermined a form of racial governance based on substantial planter autonomy. In 1865–66, southern white supremacists used their temporary control of state governments under Presidential Reconstruction to enact black codes, which, viewed from a political perspective, meant that blacks ceased to be slaves of individual masters only to become the quasislaves of the white community in general. This system required that legislation, law enforcement, and the judicial system be under exclusive white domination so that they could be used for the explicit purpose of black subjugation. A key feature was the attempt through draconian vagrancy laws to deny blacks access to a free and competitive labor market.[5]

The white monopoly of political power was overthrown when northern Republicans correctly perceived this arrangement as a new form of servitude. Congressional Reconstruction was an effort to create a political-legal framework for race relations based on common citizenship, manhood suffrage, equal protection of the laws, and the freedom of contract demanded by the "free labor" ideology. But the effort was short-lived. Using a combination of legitimate political mobilization within a competitive two-party electoral system and illegal or extralegal terror and intimidation, the Democratic-Conservative "Redeemers" gained control of one southern state government after another between 1870 and 1877 and proceeded thereafter to manipulate the electoral process to ensure that their Republican rivals had no chance of regaining power.[6]

"Redemption" did not lead to a full restoration of the racial order adumbrated in the black codes of 1865–66. For twenty to thirty years blacks continued to vote in parts of the ex-Confederacy and even elected congressmen from a handful of districts.[7] The segregation of public facilities, while extensive, remained primarily a matter of custom and extralegal white pressure.[8] Despite persistent efforts at coercion, black labor retained considerable mobility. Educational discrimination, exclusion from a range of occupations, and a biased judicial system put a low ceiling on black aspirations, preventing most blacks from engaging in any occupation except sharecropper or unskilled laborer and making them vulnerable to fraud and exploitation in those roles. But within their restricted sphere, blacks were relatively free to move about and take advantage of a competitive labor market. Although de facto peonage did exist for a time in some areas, it was the exception rather than the rule.[9]

Furthermore, the constitutional limitations placed by the Fourteenth and Fifteenth amendments on racially specific legislation meant that any laws designed primarily to keep blacks in "their place" could also be applied to poor whites. They, too, were placed at a disadvantage by enactments that strengthened the bargaining position of landlords at the expense of tenants and were liable to be disfranchised by poll taxes, secret ballots, and other restrictions on the suffrage that were justified as curbs on the black electorate.[10] Early efforts to establish segregation on common carriers often took the form of denying blacks access to first-class facilities, a policy that had them riding with lower-class whites who could not afford the first-class fare.[11] Hence, as Charles Flynn has recently pointed out in a study of Georgia, there was less than a perfect fit between the caste order of race relations and the class structure resulting from unequal access to the means of production. Reconstruction did not lay a foundation for substantive black equality, but its reforms of the American legal-constitutional system did inhibit efforts to make class and caste lines in the South coincide, as they had under slavery.[12] The segregationists of the 1890s were seeking ways to extend the caste principle and come as close as possible to a social order based clearly and consistently on white supremacy.

Tracing the antecedents of "native segregation" and apartheid in South Africa is complicated by the fact that what is now a unified state was divided into four distinct political units during the late nineteenth century. There were three differing approaches to race relations and "native affairs"—one shared, more or less, by the twin Afrikaner republics of the Transvaal and the Orange Free State, a second characterizing the British colony at the Cape of Good Hope, and a third associated with the British settlement in Natal.

The Afrikaner republics were relatively pure examples of what might be called "herrenvolk" states. Under their constitutions, formally democratic systems based on universal white manhood suffrage were established. Not only were Africans totally excluded from the franchise, they were scarcely accorded a legal existence, even as inferiors. The Africans who squatted and worked on white farms were treated at best like rightless aliens and at worst like prisoners of war. Governments sometimes demanded labor tribute from conquered African communities and distributed the workers provided among white farmers. But nothing like a centralized, state-enforced system of compulsory labor actually developed. The Afrikaner governments were notoriously weak and inefficient. Almost entirely lacking in the resources and bureaucratic structure of a modern state, they had little more than a moral authority and were virtually incapable of any activity, except perhaps waging war, that involved large expenditures and numerous functionaries. Consequently, the actual relationships between white farmers with their enormous individual holdings and the African squatters on whom they principally depended for labor were usually worked out on an ad hoc basis and often took on the character of an informal feudalism in which Africans contributed varying amounts of labor in return for occupancy rights to land for their own cattle and crops. Hence the Afrikaner farm was a virtually autonomous political unit, similar in this respect to the antebellum southern plantation.[13]

The self-governing British colony at the Cape of Good Hope, on the other hand, managed to combine the incorporation of nonwhites into a common legal and political system with a relatively effective use of that system to coerce and exploit their labor. The Cape had after 1852 a "color-blind" franchise based on a property qualification and a code of laws that was likewise supposed to apply equally to all subjects, regardless of race. But since class divisions corresponded fairly closely to racial divisions, de facto white supremacy could be maintained by traditional British devices for keeping the lower orders in their place. The property qualification for voting and officeholding excluded most nonwhites while including most whites. Allegedly "nonracial" master-servant laws containing penal sanctions for violation of labor contracts operated almost exclusively as a curb on the mobility of Coloured and African farm workers because very few whites were subject to their provisions.[14]

The Natal colony ensured white domination in a radically different fashion. It set a major precedent for the later policy of "native segregation" by confining an overwhelming African majority to large "reserves" and governing them by a separate body of "customary" law—African traditions as interpreted, amended, and applied by white magistrates. This system, however, tended to be unpopular in the white settler community because the reserves it created were sufficiently large and fertile to limit the incentive of Africans to come forth and work on white farms.[15] Reacting to a shortage of African labor, the sugar planters in the coastal regions imported indentured Indian workers beginning in the 1860s. Eventually a substantial Indian minority claimed equal rights with white settlers because of their prior status as British subjects. But the colonists, who now had virtual autonomy in their internal affairs, were resourceful in developing devices for denying the franchise and legal equality to Asian immigrants.[16] In many ways, Natal was a prime testing ground for the methods that later would become the racial policies of the South African state.

Despite the obvious differences, there were certain rough similarities in the political and ideological context of white supremacy in the South in the 1880s and in South Africa on the eve of its unification after the British victory in the Anglo-Boer War. Although whites were strongly committed to ensuring their own dominance, there was still uncertainty and disagreement on the question of precisely what policies could and should be employed for this end. In the South, there was a debate between advocates of "liberal," "conservative," and "radical" approaches to race relations and lingering fears that northern Republicans might again use federal power to protect black rights.[17] In South Africa, many whites looked forward to unification because it promised a uniform native policy for the entire region, but the experiences and traditions of the various colonies and republics provided differing models to follow. Furthermore, white settlers feared that Britain had an agenda of its own, one that would provide equal rights for nonwhites who could pass muster as "civilized" subjects of the Empire.[18]

The era of intensified government action to ensure white dominance began in the South in the 1890s and took two main forms—state and local laws requiring separation of the races in transportation and other public facilities, and restrictions on the suffrage that could be enforced in such a way as to eliminate black voting entirely.[19] The establishment in 1910 of the Union of South Africa under a constitution giving whites a virtual monopoly of political participation set the stage for a rash of legislation also meant to shore up and perpetuate white hegemony. In 1913, for example, the Native Land Act restricted the rights of Africans to own or lease land outside their designated reserves and thus gave whites exclusive possession of more than four-fifths of the land area of South Africa.[20]

In both instances the term "segregation" was applied as a general label for new policies of state-enforced discrimination. Its value was partly propagandistic; it helped to obscure the element of old-fashioned racial hierarchy in the new arrangements. The races were indeed being separated, but the obvious purpose was to strengthen white dominance and privi-

73

lege. Emphasizing the horizontal aspects of segregation and playing down its role in maintaining a vertical racial order—claiming that Jim Crow meant "separate but equal" and that Native Segregation was designed to allow each race to "develop freely along its own lines"—were ways of deflecting criticism and adjusting to the ideological climate of modern capitalism. Despite the Western world's attraction to scientific racism during this period, racial policy that conformed openly and explicitly to the master-slave model (in South Africa called *baaskap*) was an anachronism that could not be reintroduced. But segregation was more than a case of old wine in new bottles. To the extent that the state actually limited the freedom of whites as well as blacks in the new order, it went against the tendency of racial slavery or *baaskap* to give individual white masters great latitude in their dealings with nonwhite dependents. What was most obviously "modern" about segregation was its effort to bring most aspects of race relations within the domain of written law and under the authority of governmental bureaucracies.[21]

Nothing of this sort would have been possible if white supremacists in the South and South Africa had not been in control of the relevant state apparatus. In the latter case, as John Cell points out, "the crucial mechanism in the development of the persistent pattern of race and class relations called segregation was the centralized power of the South African state."[22] This state could be overtly and blatantly white-supremacist because the British government had, in its haste to accommodate white settlers and withdraw from political responsibility for South Africa, failed to carry through on promises it made before and during the Boer War to guarantee "equal rights for all civilized men" regardless of race. The American parallel was the North's "retreat from Reconstruction," which was completed in the 1890s by Congress's defeat of the Lodge proposal for federal intervention in southern elections and the notorious Supreme Court decisions authorizing segregation and disfranchisement. White southerners and South Africans were thereby empowered to implement more thoroughgoing and systematic policies of racial differentiation free of the fear that they would be overruled by a higher political authority.[23]

Local autonomy was, of course, only a precondition for legalized segregation; its actual implementation was carried out by groups within each society that expected to benefit from it in some way. Are there any significant similarities in the forces behind the new racial order in the two cases? In other words, are the two segregation movements really comparable? In *White Supremacy,* I noted the differences in the forms that segregation took and in the kinds of separation that were central to the two systems, concluding that "Jim Crow" and "Native Segregation" served different purposes and hence could not be explained in terms of a single pattern of causation. The work of Cell and Greenberg, both of whom make strong cases for a similar pattern of causation, forces a reconsideration of this issue.

Cell interprets segregation in terms of the great transformations wrought by industrialization and urbanization. In both the South and South Africa, he argues, the "vertical," face-to-face pattern of race relations appropriate to an agrarian society was simply not applicable once the forces of industrial capitalism had gained ascendency. The new system, with its commitment to "horizontal" divisions, was an effective and "modern" system of racial control when anonymous masses of blacks and whites confronted each other in cities and large-scale industries. By viewing segregation as a manifestation of the "systemic" change from premodern to modern society, Cell gives it a meaning that has theoretical and historiographic resonance. But his argument remains on a rather abstract plane and conveys only a fleeting insight into the specific motives or interests of the individuals and groups most directly responsible for the new racial policies.[24]

For Greenberg, on the other hand, intensified state action on behalf of white supremacy is attributable to the comparable influence in the two situations of specific "class actors." He is more sensitive than Cell to direct economic motivations and finds more possibility of tension between capitalist modernization and overtly racist policies. In brief, he argues that "intensification of the racial order" in South Africa and the state of Alabama took place at a particular stage of capitalist development, a time when commercial farmers were politically dominant. Commercial agriculture and primary industries such as mining—of critical importance in the early phases of industrialization—benefited directly from coercive labor policies. Consequently, farmers and mine owners used the state to hold blacks in a subservient position so that they could be exploited in ways that departed from the mature capitalist norm of "free labor." This economic interpretation of the new forms of racial dominance accounts effectively for the labor-control aspects of apartheid in South Africa, but to apply it to Alabama, Greenberg must give more weight to examples of direct labor coercion—such as convict leasing and peonage—than most economic historians would find warranted.[25]

As capitalism matured and secondary industry came to dominate the economy, he argues, a new class of businessmen without a direct stake in repressive labor systems gained increasing influence. In the case of Alabama, a shift in the economic base from agriculture and mining to a more modern form of industrial capitalism provided an opening for the civil rights movement of the 1960s. It was the business community, Greenberg argues, that reoriented the South toward racial reform and accommodation when there seemed to be no other way to restore order and prosperity to communities disrupted by racial conflict and confrontation. He suggests that South African businessmen, also less dependent than they once were on forced labor, might play a similar role in the future. A lesson that could be drawn from his analysis is that pressure on the South African economy from internal resistance and external sanctions will lead these critical "class actors" to challenge an apartheid system that no longer works to their advantage.[26]

Comparative historians in general can be divided into two camps, those like Cell and Greenberg who are looking for similarities in order to support a general theory of historical development and those who pursue differences in order to draw attention to the unique or peculiar qualities of individual societies. The two approaches are not mutually exclusive, for the "lumpers" would be totally unpersuasive if they represented two distinctive cases as identical, and the "splitters" must establish a minimal degree of commonality in order to make contrast more than obvious. Indeed, one strategy is to show that what seems different is really similar, while the other tries to uncover the differences that hide behind apparent similarities. Deciding which approach is the more fruitful and appropriate for comparing modern intensifications of white supremacy in the South and in South Africa depends ultimately on what question one wants to ask. Both Cell and Greenberg are asking how ascriptive racial inequality, allegedly a relic of premodern social systems, can be extended and accentuated by a modern capitalist state. They look at the two most conspicuous examples of this phenomenon and find that there are some factors common to both situations. But another question that might be central to a comparative inquiry is why it was that government-enforced segregation and discrimination in the southern states could be toppled by a decade or so of nonviolent protest and liberal reformism while thirty-five years of sustained and sometimes violent black resistance has so far proved incapable of compelling fundamental changes in the political foundations of white supremacy in South Africa. This question draws attention to a major variation and to the possibility that there were inherent differences in the two systems making one of them more susceptible to reform than the other. Both racial orders were consistent with capitalist development, but there may have been differences in the interrelationship of class formation, racist attitudes, and political development that will help to explain the fact that government ceased to sustain overt racial discrimination in the South without the massive upheaval that similar changes are likely to require in South Africa.

Beneath the broad similarities in impulse—the attractiveness of segregation as a means of racial control in urban-industrial settings and the interest of primary producers in limiting black rights to make their labor more exploitable—there were significant differences in the extent and character of state action for discriminatory purposes. In South Africa a sovereign unified state, in which citizenship was limited to whites, treated Africans as rightless aliens and ruled them in what can only be described as a totalitarian fashion. It seems hardly necessary any longer to describe the system of pass laws, influx controls, labor contracts, occupational color bars, and residence restrictions that sustained and—despite some recent modifications—still sustains a pattern of separate but unequal in social, economic, political, and cultural life. Although participants in a single economy, Europeans and Africans are scarcely members of the same society, and only the former belong to the constituted polity. In the South, state and local governments—subordinate units in a federal system governed by a constitution that prohibited forced labor, legal inequality, and suffrage restrictions based on race—were able through subterfuge, strained interpretations of the law, and extralegal terror or intimidation to place blacks under a form of racial tyranny. But it is no apology for Jim Crow to point out that it was less thoroughgoing and comprehensive than its South African analogue. Southern blacks were not required by law to carry passes, get official permission to relocate, live in designated areas remote from where most whites resided, engage only in menial occupations not carried on by whites, or work under contractual arrangements different from those that could be applied to employees of European descent.

All of the above requirements *did* apply to southern blacks before the Civil War, and it is a measure of the lasting impact of emancipation and Reconstruction that the kinds of restrictions on black freedom and mobility that in the American context recalled slavery were beyond the pale even at the height of the segregation era. Perhaps the greatest shortcoming in the work of "lumpers" like Cell and Greenberg is their lack of attention to the revolutionary change in the legal-political context of American race relations brought about by the Civil War and their failure to appreciate what the lack of a similar watershed has meant for the history of white supremacy in South Africa.[27]

I have no desire to play down the immense sufferings and disabilities of southern blacks between the 1880s and the 1960s. Southern white supremacists were adroit and successful in their efforts to deny substantive equality to blacks within a constitutional system that was supposed to preclude government-sanctioned racial discrimination. They used their control of state and local governments to enforce the laws in a blatantly discriminatory fashion. Election officials, applying supposedly nonracial tests, found few blacks qualified to vote; white judges and juries consistently denied equal justice to black defendants and litigants; and sheriffs and policemen enforced white supremacy within the law if possible but outside it if necessary. Furthermore, the very looseness and decentralized character of the formal racial controls, combined with the failure of the legal system to protect even the most basic rights of blacks, encouraged lynching and other forms of extralegal violence. Life under Jim Crow had special cruelties and burdens that would make any claim that it caused less individual suffering than some other system of racial oppression highly dubious.[28]

Nevertheless, southern blacks did possess one basic right, in practice as well as on paper, that distinguishes their situation in historically significant ways from that of black South Africans. If conditions became intolerable in one place, they could go somewhere else. Lack of a pass system or any other centralized control of black movement made local attempts to immobilize black sharecroppers and farm laborers relatively ineffective. Robert Higgs has argued, fairly persuasively in my view, that such mobility limited exploitation of blacks within the labor markets to which they had access.[29] It also opened a path of escape from the South itself. Migration to the North was scarcely exodus to a promised land, but it did mean a restoration of voting rights and an escape from the full rigors of Jim Crow. No similar outlet or safety valve was available to black South Africans.

One reason why the southern system of racial control was imperfect when viewed from a South African perspective was the authority of the Constitution itself; although its provisions are subject to a variety of interpretations, some of which may violate its spirit, there have been strong ideological and institutional sanctions preventing governments from doing things that it explicitly prohibits. Although late-nineteenth-century court decisions narrowed the scope of the Reconstruction amendments and made them relatively ineffectual as instruments in the struggle for black equality, limits on white-supremacist legislation remained in effect. Decisions during the height of the Jim Crow era outlawing debt peonage, "grandfather clauses" to restrict suffrage, and compulsory residential segregation provide evidence of the restraining hand of the judiciary. Militant southern white supremacists of the early twentieth century knew that their options were limited and that a sword was hanging over their heads; hence they campaigned vigorously for repeal of the Fourteenth and Fifteenth amendments. It took half a century for the sword to fall and for the amendments to be enforced in the way that their framers intended, but such a development was always possible, and the anticipation of it gave heart to black and northern liberal protest against southern segregationism.[30]

The South African constitution of 1910, on the other hand, was an explicit, unambiguous mandate for white supremacy. It ratified the prohibition or severe restriction of nonwhite suffrage already in effect in the provinces, limited membership in parliament to Europeans, and gave the all-white parliament the power to amend the constitution (except for entrenched clauses protecting Afrikaner linguistic rights and the qualified, "nonracial" suffrage in the Cape) by simple majority vote.[31] Who knows what southern segregationists would have done if they had possessed such centralized, sovereign power?

The dismantling of southern segregation, painful as it was, would have been much more difficult if it had required ending an elaborate system based explicitly on the notion that blacks had no rights that whites must respect—a system which had produced a pattern of discriminatory land allocation and labor coercion essential to the economy and requiring a massive white bureaucracy for its enforcement. Hence there is little historical basis for anticipating that apartheid can be abolished in the same reformist, nonrevolutionary fashion as Jim Crow. At the very least, overthrowing apartheid will require a radical change in the political and constitutional system. In contrast to the United States, where racial reform could occur within the existing constitutional framework and was even favored by it, the political and legal structure of South Africa is racist to the core; the aspirations of its black majority can only be fulfilled in a new polity. Not only does the electorate need to be enlarged severalfold to include black citizens, but the official borders of the country must be redrawn to include the "homelands" that have been granted nominal independence during the past decade. Nevertheless, it is possible that the abolition of legalized segregation and disfranchisement in the United States teaches some lessons that are relevant to the calculations of those working for the demise of apartheid in South Africa.

Systematic attempts to explain why Jim Crow came to an end when and how it did have not yet been made, but some of the factors are clear. The immediate cause was a rising tide of black protest that exposed the injustice of the southern racial order, threatened public order and prosperity in the region, and ultimately compelled federal intervention to implement some of the reforms demanded by black protesters. Southern whites resisted vigorously so long as the federal government was inactive or irresolute and the protests could be crushed or contained. But when faced with a dual insurrection—blacks against the southern white establishment and militant white supremacists against federal authority—moderate white leaders took charge and acquiescence to racial reform came swiftly.[32]

Among the preconditions for this scenario were the significant changes that had taken place in the respective situations of the main actors—Afro-Americans, the national political community acting through the federal government, and the southern white establishment—since the time when most people, North and South, had expected legalized segregation to last forever. Because of the great migration to the North, blacks had been, in effect, reenfranchised, and their votes became significant in northern states and in national politics. Furthermore, blacks had made substantial economic gains as a result of World War II and the rapid economic growth of the postwar years. Hence, as William J. Wilson has pointed out, an increase in the group's resources had made effective protest more likely.[33] The federal government was not only increasingly sensitive to blacks as an interest group in the electorate but also felt other pressures to implement liberal racial policies. Intellectuals and opinion makers were caught up in a revulsion to racist ideologies inspired by environmentalist social science and the horror evoked by Nazi racial policies. Not only were the white supremacist ideas no longer respectable, but the practices that they rationalized had become a liability in America's effort to exert world leadership. Jim Crow and racial unrest in the United States undercut the cold-war propaganda campaign to win "the hearts and minds of men" in Asia and in Africa.[34]

Less well understood are the preconditions for the retreat of the southern white establishment in the face of black and federal pressure in the mid-1960s. Would similar pressure have brought the same result fifty years earlier, or were basic changes in southern economic and social life required to prevent a deep sectional crisis and perhaps even a new civil war? Jonathan Weiner and Stanley Greenberg have contended that the South underwent a great transformation between the 1930s and the 1950s that reduced the stake of the South's ruling classes in a repressive racial order to the point that their vital interests no longer required its survival. The modernization of agriculture, the subsequent decline and virtual disappearance of sharecropping, and the shift of the economy's base from primary to secondary industry weakened the class basis for the whole Jim Crow system—which is apparently viewed by these historians as a scaffolding for the labor coercion required by a precapitalist or agrarian capitalist elite.[35] In my view this interpretation underestimates the noneconomic incentives for Jim Crow, exaggerates the element of direct coercion in the postbellum agricultural labor system, and posits too direct a linkage between such labor controls as existed and the laws segregating and disfranchising blacks. In the tradition of C. Vann Woodward, I view the original segregationist impulse in the South as inspired more by sociopolitical concerns than economic interests. A dominant elite—the politicians, planters, and businessmen who controlled the Democratic party—responded to the threat that lower-class white movements, especially Populism, posed to their hegemony by drawing the color line more sharply. Segregation laws substituted white status gains for economic justice, and disfranchisement precluded the kind of interracial class movement that conservatives feared.[36] If this interpretation is correct, then a main internal precondition for the success of the southern civil rights movement would be the confidence of the establishment that lower-class whites, now more likely to be industrial workers than marginal farmers, would not join with blacks in radical movements that threatened fundamental social and economic relationships. For a variety of reasons, there was no conceivable basis for such fears in the 1960s.[37]

Clearly, however, the economic tranformation of the South eased white accommodation to a new order of race relations. But I would put more stress on the South's integration into a national corporate economy than on changes in its labor system. Since 1940, in the words of Harvard Sitkoff, "power began to shift from the rural areas to the cities and from tradition-oriented landed families to the new officers and professionals in absentee-owned corporations. Industrialization also accelerated urbanization and the migration to the South of millions of white-collar workers and their families who had little stake in the perpetuation of the rural color-caste system."[38] In an age of chain stores and interstate or even multinational enterprises, the southern business community could not act independently of national corporate interests, even if it wished to do so. When the top brass of corporate America decided that Jim Crow had to go, as it in effect did in 1963, local managers and executives had to go along.[39]

Can anything resembling this scenario be anticipated in South Africa, despite the obvious differences in the political and constitutional framework for reform? Black dissatisfaction and protest is the principal common denominator, and the major variable is the responsiveness of the white community to the black struggle for equality. One might hypothesize that a combination of external and internal pressure sufficient to frighten ruling whites with the prospect of severe economic loss and massive public disorder—a rough approximation of what happened in Birmingham and some other southern cities—would compel major concessions. But the analogy should be tempered by a realization that South African whites have a much greater stake in apartheid than southern whites of the 1960s had in Jim Crow. Enfranchising Africans would create an overwhelming black majority, that majority would undoubtedly initiate reforms of the labor system that could cause a substantial increase in black wages at the expense of white wages and profits, and the ethnic monopoly of political power currently enjoyed by Afrikaners would abruptly cease.[40] The tangible privileges that whites currently enjoy are enormous and of a kind not readily sacrificed. Nonviolent resistance could work in the South, but has proved ineffective or even suicidal in the South African context,[41] and the international community obviously lacks the cohesion, the will, and the legal basis to intervene directly in the way that the United States government did in the southern states. Hence the abolition of apartheid entails a struggle inevitably more violent, disruptive, and revolutionary than the American civil rights movement needed to be.

In conclusion, I would hazard the opinion that a reformist solution following the southern model is becoming increasingly unlikely but is not impossible. Recent events suggest that economic sanctions and intensifying black protest would induce business and corporate leaders to throw their weight behind major reforms. The government, although it is no mere creature of the business community but has more the character of an Afrikaner ethnic machine, is susceptible to business pressure to some degree and would clearly have to take drastic action if it could no longer govern and guarantee the physical security of the white population. Hence some kind of gradual process leading to black majority rule is not inconceivable. This is the solution that Western liberals should work for, and its success would be more likely if the proposals for disinvestment, boycott, and embargo currently being advanced by the antiapartheid movement achieved a greater measure of success.

But I fear that it may already be too late for a reformist solution. Black leaders might well refuse to cooperate in a gradual sharing of power even if the government proposed it in good faith. In other words, polarization may be at or nearing the point of creating a classic revolutionary situation, a zero-sum struggle that will plunge South Africa into a prolonged race and class war. The death of apartheid would thus turn out to be very different from Jim Crow's demise. Unfortunately, comparative analysis lends more support to that prospect than to the one that American liberals would prefer. For myself, I hope that apartheid does not have to be drowned in blood, as southern slavery was, but I find insufficient evidence to sustain a more optimistic prognosis.

Notes

1. George M. Fredrickson, *White Supremacy: A Comparative Study in American and South African History* (New York, 1981); John W. Cell, *The Highest Stage of White Supremacy: The Origins of Segregation in South Africa and the American South* (Cambridge, Eng., 1982); Stanley B. Greenberg, *Race and State in Capitalist Development* (New Haven, 1980). My book deals with the United States as a whole, and Greenberg uses the state of Alabama rather than the South as a whole as his American unit for comparison with South Africa. He also includes brief discussions of ethnic conflict in Israel and Northern Ireland. Only Cell focuses explicitly and exclusively on the South and South Africa, but the other works make this comparison either by extension or out of recognition that the South was the part of the United States in which the white-supremacist impulse was most fully institutionalized.

2. Greenberg surveys the vast body of social theory that is based on this assumption. *Race and State*, 6–12.

3. Ibid., 12–22. See also Guy Hunter, ed., *Industrialisation and Race Relations: A Symposium* (London, 1965); Oliver Cromwell Cox, *Caste, Class, and Race: A Study in Social Dynamics* (New York, 1959); and Donald L. Horowitz, *Ethnic Groups in Conflict* (Berkeley, 1985).

4. This view of the plantation as a miniature state was apparently first set forth by the proslavery writer Robert L. Dabney in *A Defense of Virginia* (New York, 1867). See especially pp. 28–30.

5. See Theodore B. Wilson, *The Black Codes of the South* (University, Ala., 1965).

6. Recent works differ in the importance they assign to party mobilization and terror in the Redemption process. The former is stressed by Michael Perman in *Road to Redemption: Southern Politics, 1869–1879* (Chapel Hill, 1984). The latter is highlighted by Ted Tunnell in *Crucible of Reconstruction: War, Radicalism, and Race in Louisiana, 1862–1877* (Baton Rouge, 1984).

7. For a recent case study of one district where blacks retained political influence long after Reconstruction, see Eric Anderson, *Race and Politics in North Carolina, 1872–1901: The Black Second* (Baton Rouge, 1981).

8. C. Vann Woodward. *The Strange Career of Jim Crow*, 3d rev. ed. (New York, 1974); Howard N. Rabinowitz, *Race Relations in the Urban South, 1865–1890* (New York, 1978); Fredrickson, *White Supremacy*, 260–62.

9. This view of the economic situation of blacks in the postbellum South is based on what strike me as the best-supported and most plausible arguments in Robert Higgs's controversial *Competition and Coercion: Blacks in the American*

Economy, 1865–1914 (Cambridge, Eng., 1977). I agree with Higgs's claim that most blacks had physical mobility and that wages and tenancy agreements were more responsive to market pressures than to racial prejudice. But I would put more emphasis than he does on the larger pattern of discrimination that disadvantaged blacks at the starting line of economic competition and also blocked their access to skilled and well-paying occupations.

10. On creeping suffrage restriction and its effect on whites, see J. Morgan Kousser, *The Shaping of Southern Politics: Suffrage Restriction and the Establishment of the One-Party South, 1880–1910* (New Haven, 1974), 1–138.

11. Fredrickson, *White Supremacy,* 261.

12. Charles L. Flynn, Jr., *White Land, Black Labor: Caste and Class in Late Nineteenth Century Georgia* (Baton Rouge, 1983).

13. Fredrickson, *White Supremacy,* 177–79; Stanley Trapido, "Reflections on Land, Office and Wealth in the South African Republic, 1850–1900," in Shula Marks and Anthony Atmore, eds., *Economy and Society in Pre-Industrial South Africa* (London, 1980), 350–68.

14. Fredrickson, *White Supremacy,* 181–85; Stanley Trapido, " 'The Friends of the Natives': Merchants, Peasants, and the Ideological Structure of Liberalism in the Cape, 1854–1910," in Marks and Atmore, *Economy and Society,* 247–74.

15. Fredrickson, *White Supremacy,* 185–86; David Welsh, *The Roots of Segregation: Native Policy in Natal, 1845–1910* (Cape Town, 1971).

16. See Robert A. Huttenback, *Racism and Empire: White Settlers and Colored Immigrants in the British Self-Governing Colonies, 1830–1910* (Ithaca, 1976), 52–58, 139–54, 195–240.

17. For differing formulations of this division on racial policy, see Woodward, *Strange Career,* 31–65, and Joel Williamson, *The Crucible of Race: Black-White Relations in the American South Since Emancipation* (New York, 1984), 79–139.

18. Fredrickson, *White Supremacy,* chapter 4 passim.

19. Woodward, *Strange Career,* 67–109.

20. Cell, *Highest Stage,* 79–80; Fredrickson, *White Supremacy,* 239–42.

21. Cell, *Highest Stage,* passim.

22. Ibid., 65.

23. Fredrickson, *White Supremacy,* 179–98.

24. Cell, *Highest Stage.* See especially pp. 1–20, 131–229.

25. Greenberg, *Race and State.* The thesis is summed up on pp. 391–96 and the interpretation of Alabama's economy in the New South era is developed on pp. 107–119, 213–32. For a summary and analysis of the views of economic historians on the labor system of the South in this period, see Harold D. Woodman, "Sequel to Slavery: The New History Views the Postbellum South," *Journal of Southern History* 47 (November 1977): 523–54. Woodman takes issue with the efforts of new economic historians like Robert Higgs to explain the situation of blacks in terms of the operation of a classical market economy, but he is also critical of the school of Marxist historians who see sharecropping as

the survival of a precapitalist form of labor control. His own argument for the gradual proletarianization of black labor does not require as much stress as Greenberg places on the direct coercion of labor in ways that are alien to the normal practices of an industrial capitalist economy.

26. Greenberg, *Race and State*, 176–208, 232–42.

27. See Fredrickson, *White Supremacy*, 238.

28. Higgs effectively sums up the de facto vulnerabilities of blacks in a legal and political order controlled by white supremacists: "During the period 1865–1914, the legislation of the southern states probably mattered less than the refusal of the whites who controlled the legal machinery to provide equal protection to the blacks. This allowed a reign of 'private' lawlessness, intimidation, and violence." *Competition and Coercion*, 10.

29. Ibid., 75–77, 93, 119 passim. See also Gavin Wright, *Old South, New South: Revolutions in the Southern Economy Since the Civil War* (New York, 1986), chap. 4.

30. See Fredrickson. *White Supremacy*, 197–98, 235, 254.

31. The definitive work on the making of South Africa's white-supremacist constitution is Leonard M. Thompson, *The Unification of South Africa, 1902–1910* (Oxford, 1960).

32. My treatment of the civil rights movement and southern desegregation draws on Harvard Sitkoff, *The Struggle for Black Equality, 1954–1980* (New York, 1981).

33. William J. Wilson, *Power, Racism, and Privilege: Race Relations in Theoretical and Sociohistorical Perspectives* (New York, 1973), 122–27.

34. George M. Fredrickson, *The Black Image in the White Mind* (Middletown, Conn., 1987), 330–31; Sitkoff, *Black Struggle*, 16–17.

35. Jonathan M. Wiener, "Class Structure and Economic Development in the American South," *American Historical Review* 84 (October 1979), 987–91; Greenberg, *Race and State*, 241–42. Harold Woodman effectively criticizes Wiener's view that the postbellum South had a "system of 'bound' labor" in his comment on the AHR article (p. 999).

36. In my view, the main lines of Woodward's classic interpretation of the impetus behind the movements for Jim Crow and disfranchisement, as set forth in *Strange Career*, remain more persuasive than any alternative explanation so far advanced.

37. I have in mind such factors as the weakness of organized labor in the South, the pervasive anticommunism and antiradicalism of the period, and the lack of evidence that lower-class whites had a disposition to cooperate with blacks in movements for social and economic reform.

38. Sitkoff, *Black Struggle*, 15.

39. Ibid., 155.

40. In 1977, 35 percent of all employed Afrikaners worked for the state, either directly as civil servants or for state-owned enterprises. Government employment has been a principal means for Afrikaner advancement since the time

when this group had a massive "poor white" problem in the 1920s. Dismantling apartheid would automatically cost Afrikaners many jobs by eliminating the vast bureaucracy that "separate development" entails. Loss of majority political power would mean that nonwhites could compete for the remaining positions. See Heribert Adam and Hermann Giliomee, *Ethnic Power Mobilized: Can South Africa Change?* (New Haven, 1979), 160–76, 221–32.

41. Efforts at massive civil disobedience in the "defiance campaign" of 1951–52 and again in 1960 were met with such a draconian response that this form of protest had to be abandoned. After approximately seventy nonviolent demonstrators were shot down by the police at Sharpeville in 1960, the black resistance movement was forced to accept limited violence as an essential tactic in the struggle against apartheid.

How Black Was Rhett Butler?

Joel Williamson

One of the striking paradoxes in American literature is that Margaret Mitchell was born into a social universe that was obsessed with blackness, and yet she wrote a novel that seemed so totally white.

Sam Hose

In April 1899, a year and a half before Margaret Mitchell was born in Atlanta, a black man named Sam Hose was lynched in nearby Newnan. All over America, people knew about the lynching. Hose was a farm worker who had allegedly killed his erstwhile employer, Alfred Cranford, at the supper table with an axe. As white newspapers told the story, he then searched the house for money but found only a few Confederate dollars. Apparently in a rage, he returned to the kitchen and raped Mattie Cranford on the floor next to the still-warm body of Alfred Cranford, "literally within arm-reach," the newspapers said, "of where the brains were oozing from her husband's head." These shocking details come from the Atlanta *Constitution,* which got it from a friend of the family, who got it, so he claimed, from Mrs. Cranford herself. The *Constitution* was even able to report Hose's words as he left the scene of the crime. "Now I am through with my work," he reputedly said, "let them kill me if they can." The *Constitution*'s rival, the Atlanta *Journal,* altered the words to have the departing Hose declare: "I have done now what I have always wanted to do."[1]

Ten days later Sam Hose was caught near Macon and returned to be lynched in the community where the crime had occurred. On the afternoon of the lynching, people standing on street corners in Atlanta discussed a fitting punishment for Hose. The *Constitution* reported that they agreed that hanging was not enough.[2] White Atlanta had no need for concern that Hose's punishment would be less awful than his supposed crime.

After his capture, the lynchers took Hose to a confrontation with Mrs. Cranford's mother in Newnan, Mrs. Cranford herself being in a state of collapse. This was in accord with the ritual of lynching that had been built up in the South over the preceding decade. The ostensible purpose was to secure a positive identification of the criminal. Then the party marched down the road in a procession toward the Cranford farm. Hose, the "black beast," as he was sometimes called by the press, led the column. He was closely guarded and held in check by a rope leash. Behind him followed several hundred men, and these, in turn, were followed by, as the Macon *Telegraph* reported, "a line of buggies and vehicles of all kinds, their drivers fighting for position in line."[3] The procession never got to the Cranford farm. Fearing interference from the governor's agents, the lynchers turned off the road into a clearing in the piney woods. In the middle of the clearing, there was a single young tree stout enough to use as a stake. Hose was stripped and chained to the tree. Knives were brought out. Ceremoniously, one act after another, one ear was cut off, then the other, then fingers. Finally, they worked down to cut away the man's genitals. After further preparations, a fire was set under Hose's feet, individuals in the crowd having carried some fifteen cords of firewood from a neighboring farm. It was a slow fire, and as the agony proceeded the lynchers sometimes took burning wood away from the fire to prolong the process. Possibly they wanted Hose to suffer in precisely equal measure as they imagined Mrs. Cranford had suffered. This, too, was according to the ritual of lynching. While a cadre of activists proceeded with the torture of Hose, hundreds of people watched, sometimes so silently that only the crackling fire could be heard. At other times, one journalist declared, "instead of pity, there was mirth and merriment at every wild contortion." Yet, as the *Constitution* said, "Many of those present turned away from the sickening sight, and others could hardly look at it."[4] Even as the fire cooled, members of the mob moved in to take pieces of the body as relics—large bones, then small, teeth, and finally slices of heart and liver. And some took portions of the ashes themselves wrapped in handkerchiefs. The tree that had served as a stake was chopped down and taken, some thought, to Atlanta.[5]

The next morning a delegation of citizens came out from Newnan to gather up the remaining ashes and bury them. The stump of the tree was cut off level with the ground. Soon there was no trace of what had happened there, and local whites declared they could again sleep peacefully at night.[6]

Margaret Mitchell

Margaret Mitchell was born in November 1900. She was born white and into the elite of the Atlanta world. She was born, in fact, in her grandmother's house on Cain Street in an old and affluent part of the city. Her grandmother, Annie Fitzgerald Stephens, was born into the planter element. Annie's father was an Irish Catholic immigrant who before the war owned thirty-five slaves and two thousand acres near Jonesboro in Clayton County. Annie married into wartime Atlanta, survived the great fire of September 1864, the remainder of the war, and Reconstruction, and then outlived her successful businessman husband by many years. Annie's daughter, Maybelle, married a promising young lawyer, Eugene Mitchell. Soon after Margaret was born, Maybelle moved her family into a large Victorian house around the corner on Jackson Street. Maybelle was an ardent suffragette and headed a militant faction among Atlanta's women. As a small child, Margaret used to watch from the head of the stairs while her mother preached fervent sermons on women's rights to gatherings in the living room below. One of her most vivid childhood memories was of her mother taking her to a suffrage rally presided over, as she recalled, by Carrie Chapman Catt. Wearing a ribbon around her stout little middle that read "Votes for Women," Margaret sat on the platform while her red-haired mother orated with her usual outraged passion against inequities suffered by her sex.[7]

In early youth, Margaret Mitchell lived in a Georgia possessed by racial extremism, one manifestation of which was violence perpetrated by mobs of white people upon black. Behind the violence was the conviction, rising in the minds of whites in the black belts of the South, that black people freed from the beneficent restraints of slavery a generation before were reverting to the savage state natural to their African origins. The decline was signalized most clearly by the "outrage" of white women by black men. In the decade before Margaret was born, a black person was lynched in the South at the rate of very nearly one every other day. Three years before Margaret's birth, Rebecca Latimer Felton, a leading Georgia feminist later to become the first woman to take a seat in the United States Senate, had declared to the annual meeting of the Georgia Agricultural Society on Tybee Island that white men must protect their women from retrogressing black men. "If it takes lynching to protect woman's dearest possession from drunken, raving human beasts," she cried, "then I say lynch a thousand a week if it becomes necessary." In December 1898 Felton recalled her Tybee Island speech and asserted proudly that hundreds of "good, true men cheered me to the echo."[8]

When white leaders opposed the lynchers, they soon found themselves ineffectual or overrun. Margaret was still a toddler when Andrew Sledd, a professor at nearby Emory College, published in the prestigious northern journal the *Atlantic Monthly* a head-on assault against lynching. Lynching was murder, he said, and he implicitly raised the idea that in reality the beasts in these proceedings were white, not black. Within a few months Sledd resigned and shipped off to Yale to take his doctorate, financed by a thousand-dollar "adjustment" in pay. The happy ambience of his exile almost surely sprang from the fact that he was the son-in-law of the most powerful Southern Methodist bishop, Warren A. Candler. It might have helped, too, that Sledd's wife was the niece of Asa Candler, the founder of the Coca-Cola Company and, even then, an Emory benefactor of considerable importance.[9]

Interracial violence in the South reached a new high plateau in Margaret Mitchell's own Atlanta in September 1906 when white people of all classes ended an imagined "epidemic of rape" of white women by black men in an orgy of violence that is as yet probably unmatched in kind and horror in the history of black-white relations in America.[10] Margaret was almost six when the Atlanta riot occurred. At the time she lived with her father, mother, and older brother Stephens on Jackson Hill, immediately to the east of downtown Atlanta. Between Jackson Hill and the center of town the land dips downward into a shallow valley. In the early twentieth century, Atlanta blacks lived there, in an area that whites called "Darktown."

Margaret Mitchell's mother was visiting friends and relatives in New York at the time the riot occurred. Margaret had remained at home with her father and brother. Probably her grandmother, whose house was just around the corner, had come to stay while Maybelle was in New York. On Sunday, after the first phase of the riot had run its course on Saturday night, Eugene wrote to Maybelle. "Atlanta has had one of the most terrible nights in its history," he began. All during the summer Atlanta newspapers had whipped white fears up to the brink of hysteria, and a prolonged gubernatorial campaign had just produced a victory for extreme racism. Eugene had observed the "increasing feeling of the past few days," and the afternoon papers on Saturday "had accounts of two more assaults" by black men on white women. As he came home he saw unusually large crowds, but thought little of it. He went to bed early, but awoke about midnight. He "heard pistol shots in the distance" every few minutes, and the fire bell rang; still he was not alarmed and went back to sleep in an hour or so. He was surprised by the morning news "that 16 negroes had been killed and a multitude had been injured." The mob, Eugene learned, "numbered 10,000 and killed or tried to kill every negro they saw." In his own household, "the cook Estelle came in late and said that her brother had been all cut up." In the streets, he told his wife, "it will not do to express opinions too freely about the action of the mob in falling on inoffending negroes, for every man you meet justifies it and is enraged." After Eugene had arrived home Saturday evening, the newspapers published two sets of extras, each shouting that another white woman had been assaulted by a black man. Thereafter, he reported, "men got their guns and went to town." Sunday morning he saw the Georgia militia patrolling the streets, and things seemed quiet. Blacks were terrified, he declared, and "all keeping close."

Eugene tried to reassure Maybelle. He urged her to stay in New York and enjoy herself thoroughly. Her mother and the children were well, he said, and while he feared that the riot would break loose again that night, "there is no danger to a white man who keeps out of the mob."[11]

On the following Tuesday, Eugene was still anxious and thought another outbreak likely. "The excitement about the mob has not abated any," he wrote Maybelle. "The negroes have nearly all quit work and are hiding at home and the white people have been buying arms and ammunition to such an extent that the military have stopped the sale." Again he assured her that those who stayed at home and kept off the streets at night were in no danger. "If anything in the situation should develope to make the situation grow tenser, I will have your mother take the children down the country." He meant down to the countryside near Jonesboro where the Fitzgeralds still had relatives.[12]

On Saturday, September 29, a week after the rioting began, Eugene wrote to Maybelle again. The danger had passed, he said, and while they had kept Margaret at home "all the time," they had allowed Stephens to go to school by a safe route on the streetcars. Like racial conservatives generally in this era, Eugene deplored riotous violence but welcomed an increase in industriousness and respect for white people among blacks. He found that "negroes are taking off their hats who never knew they had hats before." His handyman Gus was now busily at work putting up a fence for him, and Henry Crawford, who "had not touched my excavating when the riot came," was now ready to go to work. Still, Eugene declared that he would not go through the "negro settlements after dark" and thought there were white sections in Atlanta where a passing black would be "rocked or beaten."

Feeling relatively secure, Eugene wrote Maybelle more fully of the fear that had seized the white community during the previous week:

Now that the reign of terror has passed, I can confess that the whole thing has been far worse than the newspapers and dispatches to Northern papers have made it out. Not so much in the actual physical violence (although that was awful enough) but in the awful terror that seized the whole town. A thousand rumors were rife that negro mobs had been poised to burn the town, cut the water pipes &c. Sunday night the rumors came thick and fast that Jackson Hill would be burned that night and Slaton and Carroll went down the street warning every man to get his gun and be ready at a moments warning. I had no gun and could only get the axe and waterkey [a T-shaped metal tool made to control the house's water supply, but that might be used as a weapon like a hatchet or pickaxe] when Margaret suggested that Mr Daleys sword would be a good thing. I adopted the suggestion. Just after dark the electric lights went out—the negroes had cut the wire in darktown. Your mother and Annie and the children went to bed and I sat up until about two o'clock and nearly all the other men in the neighborhood sat up. At about ten o'clock a detachment of soldiers came out and stayed awhile but soon left & went down into darktown. Throughout the night pistols and guns would be frequently fired off down in the dip & over about Randolph St.[13]

Clearly, Margaret Mitchell, almost six, was present at the Atlanta riot and highly conscious of the danger perceived by her father. With the verve and imagination that marked her late life, she aided positively in arming her father for the defense of the Mitchell household from attack by blacks. Eugene, bereft of gun, could only think of the axe and the waterkey, but Margaret thought of "Mr Daleys sword." Readers of *Gone With the Wind* will immediately think of "the bummer scene" where Melanie, feeble from just having given birth to Beau and fled burning Atlanta, is upstairs making valiant preparations to use Charles Hamilton's sword against the Yankee bummer should he get past Scarlett's pistol on Tara's stairway.

Just as the leading citizens of Newnan hastened to erase vestiges of the Hose lynching, the leading citizens of Atlanta worked to erase the horrors of the riot. Fairly soon, they decided that the riot had been perpetrated, not really by themselves, but rather by the lower elements of both races, and even those folks had done it under the influence of drink. With Georgia legally dried up, as it was within a year, with ignorant blacks disfranchised, as they were, legally, within another year, with compulsory public education and hence socialization for all the children of the lower elements, Atlanta again could sleep nights and progress during the day.[14]

Indeed, during the decade following the Atlanta riot white southerners seemed to flee, almost pell-mell, not merely from the recognition of the image of the black beast rapist, but even from the memory of the image. It was as if they were determined to forget the waves of lynching that swept over the South in and after 1889 and the riots that came in and after 1898. When little Mary Phagan was murdered in an Atlanta pencil factory in 1913, black suspects were passed over almost compulsively to decide that the culpable beast was factory manager Leo Frank. Frank was Jewish, New York northern, college-educated, opera-going, and, most of all, a factory-running alien to southern culture. He was convicted primarily on the testimony of the black janitor in the building, who probably had himself killed the girl and who swore that Frank was "not built like other men"—that he was, in a word, perverted. In 1915 Frank was lynched near the site of little Mary's birth, much as if he were the black beast rapist of myth. The lynch mob was moved to act at that particular time by the recent decision of the governor to commute Frank's sentence from death to life in prison. Interestingly for our story, that governor was John M. Slaton, one of the two men who had circulated among their neighbors on Jackson Hill on that Sunday in 1906, urging the men to arm themselves. In 1915, too, the second Ku Klux Klan began with the burning of a cross atop Stone Mountain, its animus against Jews, Catholics, and aliens of all kinds all but eclipsing its hatred of blacks.[15]

Amidst all of this, Margaret Mitchell, bright, engaged, and highly literate, was coming of age in Georgia. At one point in the process, perhaps when she was in her early teens, she organized the children in her neighborhood to offer a play that she had adapted from Thomas Dixon's novel *The Traitor.* Significantly, she chose herself to play the part, not of the hero, but of the traitor, a New South southerner out of an old family who, as head of the local Klan and about to be persecuted by the federals, turns rat and tells all. In 1936, after *Gone With the Wind* had appeared, Dixon wrote to Mitchell applauding her work as "the great American novel." She replied graciously, thanking him and adding that she "was practically raised on your books and love them very much."[16] Dixon had begun to write novels in 1902 for the explicit purpose of explaining to America that the white South was facing a black population that, freed from the necessarily tight restraints of slavery, was rapidly retrogressing to the bestial state. Black men would assault white women, and white men would inevitably lynch them. The first of his novels, *The Leopard's Spots,* was an instant popular and commercial success, reputedly selling a million copies. The second of the three that he wrote dealing with race and Reconstruction was *The Clansman,* which appeared in 1905. Dixon immediately turned *The Clansman* into a play, and that too was a success. In 1905 Dixon brought the performance to Atlanta, where it played to a wildly enthusiastic audience and the author himself appeared onstage after the production to explain its truth as history. Thereafter, Dixon also produced plays adapted from *The Traitor* and his novel *The Sins of the Father,* the latter a melodramatic story about the perils of interracial love and sex where the black partner is virtually indistinguishable from a white woman. Finally, *The Clansman* became the basic story for D. W. Griffith's film *The Birth of a Nation,* which played in Atlanta in 1915.[17]

It is clear that Mitchell knew Dixon's books, but we do not know whether she saw his plays or *The Birth of a Nation.* On the other hand, we know that she was avid for drama and the stage. As a student in Washington Seminary, an exclusive school for Atlanta's girls, she was highly active in the drama club. By that time her father, Eugene, was modestly prosperous as a copyright and real estate lawyer, and the family had moved to an imposing columned mansion on Peachtree Street. If Margaret failed to attend the theater to see a Dixon play or *The Birth of a Nation,* it was not for lack of either willingness or the price of a ticket.[18]

In the fall of 1918, shortly before she turned eighteen, Margaret went off to Smith College in Massachusetts—into the very heartland of the Yankee empire. Probably she went to Smith to please her mother. Her mother had rued that she herself had not pursued an interest in science to become something of a southern Madame Curie, and she was determined that her only daughter would have no such regrets. Once, when Margaret was not doing well at her studies, Maybelle took her on a ride down through the plantation country from which Annie Fitzgerald had come. She pointed out some plantations that had recovered and others that had failed. The failed plantations had belonged to weaklings, she lectured, while the Fitzgeralds and others had had the courage, the energy, and the will to survive and progress.

As best she could, Margaret gave her mother what she wanted. She went off to Smith, promising to prepare herself for medical school, after which she would go to Vienna to study under Sigmund Freud. At Smith, she ranked as only an average scholar, but was well liked by the circle of girls with whom she became friends. Particularly, they admired her "smoking skills" and the truly amazing talent she had for bringing interesting young men to campus. That talent she had exercised well in Atlanta after American entry into the war in Europe. She made a speciality of inviting whole flocks of brand-new young officers to the big house on Peachtree Street. Margaret was very petite, very attractive, and most of all very vivacious and flirtatious, and several of the soldiers announced their love of her. But she came especially to like a young New Yorker just out of Harvard named Clifford Henry. Clifford was sensitive, cultured, and, as Margaret's schoolmates thought, slightly effeminate. When Margaret went off to Smith, Clifford was in France, and they carried on a heavy correspondence until he died on October 16, 1918, of wounds incurred in battle. All of this left her friends at Smith slightly in awe of her.[19]

In January 1919 Maybelle died of influenza. After a spiritless spring semester, Peggy, as Margaret now called herself, came home to become the woman in her father's house. Eugene Mitchell had graduated from the University of Georgia in 1885, had begun to practice law and deal in Atlanta real estate the following year, and was rapidly rising in income and wealth until the Panic of 1893 and ensuing depression brought a dramatic reverse in his fortunes. Thereafter, according to his son, he was a very cautious man, perhaps overly so, and it was Maybelle who was the driving force in the family. For two years Peggy had a frustrating time attempting to run her father's house. He was totally dispirited by Maybelle's death, and his income was not nearly so high as Peggy had thought.[20]

Peggy also had severe difficulties taking the place in Atlanta society to which she was born. In 1920 she was persuaded to join that world formally as a debutante. In the process of "coming out," however, she so offended the matrons of Atlanta that they refused her the usual sequel— an invitation to join the Junior League, an honor that signaled the arrival and acceptance of a young woman into the city's elite. In part, that refusal stemmed from Peggy's having performed at one of the debutante affairs a very physical "Apache dance" in revealing attire with a sultry looking Georgia Tech student. This pattern of behavior had marked Peggy's life previously, and it would continue to do so. It seemed that she was not contented with joining southern white society and living by its rules, but also she was not willing to leave it. Her difficulty, apparently, sprang directly from her rebellion against the role assigned to her sex.[21]

In September 1922 Margaret Mitchell married Berrien K. Upshaw, a man half a year younger than she. "Red" Upshaw came from a respectable family, but he had a spotty reputation. Upshaw was six-two, square-jawed, cleft-chinned, and muscular. Friends described him as masterful, dashing, and wild. He had left the Naval Academy in Annapolis twice, enrolled in the University of Georgia in Athens at least once, and supposedly played football for the university. Peggy met him in 1920 at an Atlanta Country Club masquerade ball. He came as a pirate, and she as a pantalooned antebellum girl. When they married, he had no certain job, yet he sported rolls of money and roared around in high-powered, brightly colored cars. Rumor had it that he bootlegged moonshine out of the Georgia mountains. Certainly he drank a lot of that commodity, and so did Peggy and their friends. When Red drank, acquaintances later said, he was liable to insist upon sexual satisfaction or turn violent—or both.[22]

Clearly, Peggy was powerfully attracted to Red Upshaw. Further, she had tuned her talents for flirting and teasing to a high pitch—almost too high. Sometimes, as she said to the sister of John Marsh, her second and lasting husband, her coquetry led to the tabling of questions of seduction and "rape became more to the point." With most men, she could turn "all righteous indignation" at the crucial moment and maintain control. But Red Upshaw she had to marry. The marriage began to fail on the honeymoon when she told Red about Clifford Henry and began to correspond again with Henry's parents, marking specially the fourth anniversary of his death. Back in Atlanta, the marriage lasted barely three months. On one occasion Red assaulted his wife in front of guests. In December 1922 he left.[23]

John March, a gentle, intelligent mutual friend, picked up the pieces. He pressed Peggy into winning a reporting job on the Sunday magazine of the Atlanta *Journal*. Quickly she rose to become its most popular feature writer. John had first come to Atlanta from his native Kentucky to work as a copy editor for the Associated Press. For a time he shared quarters with Red Upshaw. He went away after Peggy's marriage to Red, but after the separation he returned. In order to be close to Peggy, he took a position in the advertising department of the Georgia Power and Light Company. Steadily, John edited Peggy's work, always criticizing and always encouraging. In the spring of 1923 she did a highly successful article on the Confederate monument that Gutzon Borglum was about to carve into the side of Stone Mountain. The monument was to consist of the faces of five Georgia generals. The wife of one of these, Mary Benning, proved to be precisely one of those brave Confederate women that Annie Fitzgerald represented and that Peggy's mother so admired. Peggy persuaded her editor to allow her to do a story on four other very strong Georgia women. The most ladylike of these was Rebecca Felton. Three others were plain women of the Old South, including one, Lucy "Bill" Kenny, who had passed as male to fight for two years as a soldier in the Army of Northern Virginia in order to be alongside her husband. When her husband was killed, she announced herself and brought his body home. One of the other women had shot to death a Tory who invaded her house during the Revolutionary War, and still another was a Cherokee princess, an "untamed savage" who had successively married three white men, and, presumably, exhausted them all. Margaret Mitchell's choice of Georgia heroines did not meet with general approval. Calling Peggy into his office to see the hate mail piled high on his desk, her editor put a stop to further such ventures in his magazine.[24]

On July 4, 1925, Independence Day, having divorced Red Upshaw,

Margaret Mitchell married John Marsh. He encouraged her to write a novel. Early in 1926 she tried one in the Jazz Age style, featuring a very strong young woman. But the hero soon became Red Upshaw and she quit. In the spring John got a raise and Peggy resigned her job. She would stay home with her maid, Lulu, in their tiny apartment and write. John still pressed her to attempt a novel. Finally, in the fall, she began. She wrote a novella that John did not like and advised that she put aside. The following week she suffered an accident in her car and for several months was incapacitated. One evening John brought home a stack of copy paper for her. The message was clear, and the next day Peggy began to write. She had elements of a story in mind, but only the vaguest notion of how it would develop. As she always did in her Sunday magazine articles, she began at the end. "She had never understood either of the men she loved and so she lost them both," she wrote.[25]

How Black Was Rhett Butler?

Margaret Mitchell grew up in a white Georgia world very much pervaded by a fear of the black beast rapist. And yet in *Gone With the Wind* there is no potential black rapist worthy of mention in more than a few lines, and none at all important enough to be given a name. Indeed, there are no really self-interested, self-moving blacks at all in the story. Some blacks are badly used by scalawags and carpetbaggers, but the most important black people—like Mammy, Pork, Dilcey, Big Sam, and Peter—are well used by elite southern whites to keep the white world in good running order. In the mass, in *Gone With the Wind*, black people are simply shunted aside. There is no hint that Atlanta University and other black schools existed during much of the time period covered by the novel, nor that there was an emerging black elite in the city. Margaret Mitchell wrote a strikingly white novel, so white in fact that some of the white characters seem black. The most important of these is Rhett Butler.

Seemingly, there are four evidences, compelling in greater or lesser degree, of Rhett's blackness. The first and least important is his coloring. The second and third relate to his attitudes and behavior in matters of work and sex. The fourth relates to the author herself.

In her novel Margaret Mitchell painted Rhett Butler as exceedingly dark. Perhaps one day some patient scholar will do a description and analysis of color references to individual characters in *Gone With the Wind*. Without doubt, Rhett would be the front-runner on the dark side, with a great number of "blacks," "darks," and "swarthies" applied to him, all now and again accentuated by the whiteness of his teeth or the redness of his lips. Interestingly, at least twice he is an Indian, and once Scarlett calls him a hound, but caresses the word as she is saying it so that it sounds more like "darling." Surprisingly, the runner-up in dark coloring would probably be Melanie Wilkes, whose very name comes from the Greek word *melanos,* meaning black. Ironically, in terms of ideals Melanie is whiter than white. At the other end of the color spectrum is Ashley Wilkes, who is not only fair and blond, but represents the very essence of light. Margaret Mitchell describes him as "sunny haired."[26]

Of course, heroes in America have often been dark, perhaps even usually so, and making Rhett Butler dark does not make him black. We can move somewhat further in that direction, however, by considering Rhett's attitudes and behavior in regard to work and sex.

When Margaret Mitchell was a child in the early years of the twentieth century, there were plenty of jobs in Atlanta for black women but, relatively speaking, not many for black men. Black women could find employment in the kitchens, laundries, and nurseries of a flourishing white middle class. White Atlanta was rising with industrial and commercial development, and every white family with any pretensions at all had to have its black servant. On the other hand, factories and stores were notoriously exclusive of black men as workers—unless as low-paid, longhoured lifters, shovelers, sweepers, and menials. The best jobs in the new economic order were reserved for white men. And yet, even as black men were hard-worked in some jobs and carefully excluded from others, the myth grew among whites that black men would not work—especially young black men.[27] Narrating in *Gone With the Wind,* Mitchell herself declared that "they did not want to be workers of any kind, anywhere." Without identifying their sources of support, she asked the rhetorical question, "Why work when the belly is full?"[28] In the novel Scarlett found a solution to the problem of black idleness, a solution that the white South at large had found during Reconstruction. The solution was, of course, the convict lease system. It was a system that still throve in Georgia when Margaret was a child.

The great depression of the 1890s had indeed cut black men, frequently young black men, away from the marginal lands of the agricultural South. Often enough they drifted toward the big cities such as New Orleans, Memphis, and Atlanta. There they found a world for which they had no preparation. Like Robert Charles, the protagonist in the New Orleans riot of 1900, they went from job to job, from address to address, from name to name, and had no wife. White people, looking on from the outside, saw the floating black man as choosing the life he seemed to live. They saw him as the runaway, the Negro loose, the Negro in the woods of previous times and other places. They saw him as the "hipster-trickster," an almost precisely counterpunctual anti-Victorian male who saw himself as too smart to work and too much man for one woman to hold.[29]

Rhett Butler certainly fills that role in Margaret Mitchell's novel, and he is despised by white society for it. Rhett is the dark, mysterious, and slightly malevolent hero loose in the world. Like Red Upshaw in Mitchell's own life, he holds no job, has no profession and no clearly visible means of support—yet he has money and lots of it. Rhett is, in a sense, the "nigger loose." He is independent, cocky, and insufferably yet subtly insolent. He has an uncanny capacity for divining the thoughts of others and for popping up at the right place and time to promote his own interests.

Like the hipster-trickster, like, say, Rhinehart in Ralph Ellison's *Invisible Man,* Rhett works in the gray zone to make his fortune. For a time during the war, southerners appreciate his services, but the North calls him a traitor, smuggler, and thief. They lock him up in their jail in Atlanta, ostensibly for killing a black man. Actually, they want him to surrender his Confederate gold. If the Yankee jail in Atlanta was hell, then Rhett is a fair representation of Stackolee, the mythical black man who was so bad that when he went to hell the devil himself couldn't keep him. In some versions of the tale, the devil becomes fearful that Stackolee will unseat him and take over hell itself. In Atlanta, Rhett sends the devil scrambling and sets himself free by threatening to reveal the fact that during the war he bought contraband goods for Confederate use from high officials in Washington. Rhett emerges from jail very rich, but not at all respectable in the eyes of the Atlanta elite, even after he saves Atlanta's Ku Klux gentry from hanging.[30]

All of this changes when Bonnie is born. Rhett wants to be respectable for her sake, and, again, he knows exactly how to do it. He modestly confesses to having served in the Confederate Army, and the doubters soon find that he served valiantly. After Bonnie is born, he takes her brother Wade to the Episcopal church for Sunday's service. But, most of all, he takes a desk in the lobby of a bank in which he owns stock, and there, in plain sight of everyone, he works hard every day all day just like other Atlantans worked. At the end of the novel, when Rhett heads for his native Charleston, it appears that he intends to return to the whiteness whence he came.[31]

Rhett himself confesses that he is too much man for one woman. The fact is also implied in his long-running intimacy with Belle Watling, the madame whose house often seems to be his home. Meeting Scarlett changes his life. She is, for him, in the turn-of-the-century phrase, "the one woman." He understands her perfectly, and bends his considerable energies toward having her love him. Appearances to the contrary notwithstanding, it's not nearly so much her body that he wants as it is her heart and mind.[32] The trouble is that Scarlett is a child. She doesn't know what she wants. She suffers an adolescent yearning for total love, for physical love as well as ideal. Ashley is the object of her passion, and he seems tempted. But Scarlett is her mother's child, and the lady inside her will not allow her to make the crucial move that would embody her feelings for him. She wants Ashley to make the first move and, hence, to assume responsibility for the acts that follow and save her from feelings of guilt. In one scene she has Ashley out of the stall and running well. She seems about to harvest the fruit of her long labors.

> "He's going to kiss me!" thought Scarlett ecstatically. "And it won't be my fault!" She swayed toward him. But he drew back suddenly, as if realizing that he had said too much—said things that he never intended to say.[33]

What Scarlett seems to want from Ashley is "no-fault sex." Ashley, of course, cannot oblige. He, too, is captive to his culture. Often he understands very well where things are, but he can't act, can't behave according to his knowledge. Like Rhett, he knows the war is lost when it begins, but goes right off to fight anyway. Rhett and Ashley are a lot alike. Rhett understands Ashley's dilemma perfectly and verbalizes it with marvelous brevity. The trouble with Ashley, Rhett says, is that "he can't be faithful to his wife with his mind or unfaithful with his body."[34] Talking southern culture, we could add, "Not only Ashley."

Scarlett has a similar problem, even after she marries Rhett. Again, Rhett understands Scarlett's problem very well. Early on in their relationship, he says, "Scarlett, you need kissing badly. That's what's wrong with you. All your beaux have respected you too much."[35] Because Rhett never pretends to be a gentleman, he is finally able to give Scarlett what he thinks she needs. In a scene that many students of *Gone With the Wind* call "the rape scene," Rhett makes a last desperate effort to possess Scarlett as a whole woman. In this instance, she has made a mess of things in another clumsy attempt to get Ashley to seduce her. Rhett is so frustrated by Scarlett's obsession with Ashley that he falls to drinking heavily in the dining room of their Peachtree Street mansion. In the southern white mind in the turn-of-the-century years, the black beast rapist was often associated with liquor. Scarlett approaches the dining room, but suddenly Rhett appears in the doorway, the light behind him, and he is "a terrifying faceless black bulk." Holding her captive in the dining room, he shows her his "large brown hands" and says, "I could tear you to pieces with them."

Placing his hands on either side of her head, he declares to Scarlett that he could smash her skull "like a walnut." Struggling, she accuses him of being a "drunken beast"; he says that she is "a child crying for the moon." Finally, Scarlett escapes.

> She ran swiftly into the dark hall, fleeing as though demons were upon her. Oh, if she could only reach her room! She turned her ankle and the slipper fell half off. As she stopped to kick it loose frantically, Rhett, running light as an Indian, was beside her in the dark. His breath was hot on her face and his hands went round her roughly, under the wrapper, against her bare skin.
>
> "You turned me out on the town while you chased him. By God, this is one night when there are only going to be two in my bed."
>
> He swung her off her feet into his arms and started up the stairs. Her head was crushed against his chest and she heard the hard hammering of his heart beneath her ears. He hurt her and she cried out, muffled, frightened. Up the stairs, he went in the utter darkness, up, up, and she was wild with fear. He was a mad stranger and this was a black darkness she did not know, darker than death. He was like death, carrying her away in arms that hurt. She screamed, stifled against him and he stopped suddenly on the landing and, turning her swiftly in his arms, bent over and kissed her with a savagery and a completeness that wiped out everything from her mind but the dark into which she was sinking and the lips on hers. He was shaking, as though he stood in a strong wind, and his lips, traveling from her downward to where the wrapper had fallen from her body, fell on her soft flesh. He was muttering things she did not hear, his lips were evoking feelings never felt before. She was darkness and he was darkness and there had never been anything before this time, only darkness and his lips upon her. She tried to speak and his mouth was over hers again. Suddenly she had a wild thrill such as she had never known; joy, fear, madness, excitement, surrender to arms that were too strong, lips too bruising, fate that moved too fast. For the first time in her life she had met someone, something stronger than she, someone she could neither bully nor break, someone who was bullying and breaking her. Somehow, her arms were around his neck and her lips trembling beneath his and they were going up, up into the darkness again, a darkness that was soft and swirling and all enveloping.[36]

Scarlett at last has found "no-fault sex." And, in a physical sense, Rhett could say: "I have done now what I have always wanted to do." But he has not won Scarlett's heart, as he always wanted, and we soon find that he went straight from Scarlett's bed to Belle's house.[37]

For Scarlett, it is the turning point in her life, and a turn for the better. With the "rape scene," she begins to become an adult, a whole person. She wakes and Rhett is gone. She sorts out her feelings. He had "used her brutally through a wild mad night and she had gloried in it." Also, she thinks, "for the first time in her life she had felt alive, felt passion as sweeping and primitive as the fear she had known the night she fled Atlanta, as dizzy sweet as the cold hate when she had shot the Yankee." She is surprised to note that she is as nervous as a bride about Rhett. "And at that idea she fell to giggling foolishly." Rhett loves her, she realizes with a thrill, and she has him at last. Now, Scarlett says to herself, "she could hold the whip over his insolent black head."[38]

Scarlett doesn't change overnight, of course, and Rhett's insolent black head does not meekly offer itself for her whipping. But Scarlett does resist the temptation to confess all about Ashley to the always-forgiving Melanie, in effect deciding to pay the tax, to bear herself the responsibility for her sins. She begins to give attention to and really care for her children. She wants to bear and to love the child who was conceived that wild night. Finally, and most important, she begins to question her ideal image of Ashley. In the end, rather tardily at age twenty-eight, she sees in Rhett some of the virtues she had imagined in Ashley and knows that she has loved him for years. Sure enough, she had never understood either of the men she loved, and so she has lost them both.[39]

But still one might hope that after she goes back to Tara and Mammy tomorrow she will indeed begin to think about it all, that she will mature enough to go on to Charleston to find both of the men she needs in Rhett, and there to find herself a whole woman—fully possessed and fully possessing.

Perhaps the most compelling evidence that Rhett Butler represents blackness comes from Margaret Mitchell's own life. During the summer of 1926, when John Marsh was pressing his housebound wife to write a novel, she passed from several years of smoking, drinking, hard working, and good health to a sequence of injuries and illnesses. She had, she said, "several hundred novels in my mind," but somehow could write none of them. [40] She procrastinated, but John persisted and in the fall she began a short story she called " 'Ropa Carmagin." Three weeks later it was a 15,000-word novella. Europa Carmagin, the heroine, is the daughter of one of those failed planter families that Margaret's mother Maybelle had warned her about, the families that did not have "gumption" enough to meet the challenges of the Civil War and Reconstruction. The Carmagin plantation offers rotting fences, exhausted fields, and a garden choked with weeds. Far from pulling renewed life from this now "barren ground," 'Ropa, as Mitchell calls her, spends her energies loving a handsome mulatto man whose mother had been a slave on the Carmagin plantation. The scene of all this is Clayton County near Jonesboro, the same as that of Tara, but the time is the 1880s, and Europa, unlike Scarlett, puts love

before money. In the end the dark lover is killed, and the neighbors force
'Ropa to leave her ancestral home.[41]

Peggy Mitchell Marsh liked Europa Carmagin and she liked the story
she had written. She thought it rich and accurate in historical detail, and
especially, she relished the idea that the theme "miscegenation" would
raise the story from "romance" to "literature." She showed the manuscript to John, as she did all she wrote, and waited for the close editing he
always supplied. John was himself fascinated by the background, the period, and he even liked Europa Carmagin. But he thought that Peggy had
not drawn a true portrait of the mulatto and that the work in general was
not up to her talent. Most of all, he did not like the theme of miscegenation. He suggested she put the manuscript aside and think about it for a
while before he attempted to make notes on it for her.[42]

In 1926, it appears that Margaret Mitchell was about to write a book
about miscegenation that was not vastly distant from the truly great novel
that William Faulkner published a decade later under the title *Absalom,
Absalom!* In that story the white girl, Judith Sutpen, loves and is fully set
to marry a mulatto man, Charles Bon, before he is shot down and killed.
Moreover, the mulatto man she would marry is her half brother—the son
of her father. We do not know who Europa's lover's father was, but we do
know that he was the son of a Carmagin slave woman. As we now understand patterns of miscegenation in the Old South, it would have been
almost ordinary if Europa's white kin had been the father of her lover, and
it would not have been unusual if her own father had been the father of
her lover.[43]

Ironically, Faulkner was finishing *Absalom, Absalom!* in the very year,
1936, that *Gone With the Wind* was published. He was in Hollywood
during much of that year and probably learned that Margaret Mitchell
was to be paid $50,000 for film rights, the most ever paid for such rights
up to that time. That knowledge might account for the value he chose to
place on screening rights for his new novel. The price was $50,000, he
wrote producer Nunnally Johnson in late October. "It's about miscegenation," he said. Faulkner's offer was refused—at any price.[44]

We cannot know exactly what was in the story of 'Ropa Carmagin.
After *Gone With the Wind* was published, Mitchell ordered her secretary
to burn the manuscript. Fortunately, the secretary made notes on the novella before she burned it, and at least three other people read the manuscript before that. Indeed, Mitchell gave the manuscript to Macmillan's
Harold G. Latham along with the manuscript of *Gone With the Wind*.
For a time after her novel was published, she apparently considered pub-
lishing the novella also. Then she decided to have it burned. Before she

died she ordered that virtually all of her papers be burned, including nearly all of the manuscript of *Gone With the Wind*, saving just enough to prove that she, and not someone else, was the real author of the novel.[45]

We do know that Margaret liked her heroine, Europa Carmagin. The name Europa carries great significance. It comes, of course, from a figure in Greek mythology. We in the West in modern times can hardly go through school without encountering a depiction of "The Rape of Europa" by some master artist. Europa was the daughter of an ancient king, a lovely, sweet girl who woke one morning from a disturbing dream. In the dream two continents in female forms struggled to possess her. One said that she had given birth to Europa and hence owned her; the other said that Zeus, the king of the gods, would deliver Europa to her. Rising, the young woman went down to the meadows by the sea to pick flowers with her girl friends, all of whom were very beautiful. Zeus, looking down from on high, was smitten by Europa and felt compelled to manifest himself to her. Hera, his wife, was away at the time, but Zeus was always careful in these matters. He came to Europa as a bull, not a plain bull but one of extraordinary beauty—chestnut colored, with a silver circle on his brow and horns crescent-shaped like young moons. So gentle and comely was he that the maidens all went about him to breathe his odors, to hear his melodious lowing, to touch him. But he came to Europa and knelt as if offering his broad back to her. She called to the others to join her in mounting him. "He is not like a bull," she said, "but like a good, true man." She sat on his back, but before the other girls could join her the bull rose and dashed out onto the sea. Miraculously the animal did not sink into the water but ran over its surface while dolphins and other creatures splashed and frolicked alongside. Momentarily Europa was frightened. With one hand she held onto one of the magnificent horns and with the other she caught up the skirts of her purple dress to keep them dry. Europa soon suspected that the gods were involved in this and said as much to the bull, begging him not to cast her off in some strange place all alone. Zeus then announced himself and said that all he did was for the love of her. He meant to take Europa to his own special island, Crete, where Hera could not harm her and where she would bear him "Glorious sons whose septres shall hold sway / Over all men on earth."[46]

Quite likely Margaret Mitchell knew the story of Europa and so named her heroine with full knowledge of its implications.[47] Yet Mitchell's Europa story ends tragically. If the mulatto hero is the bull, the bull is killed and Europa exiled both from the land that gave her birth and the happiness as a woman that her lover would afford.

Peggy was devastated by John's reaction to her Europa story. She moped about over the weekend, and on Monday, when John had gone to work, got in the car and drove out toward Jonesboro. It was raining. Surprised by a stop sign, she braked suddenly and skidded into a tree. Luckily she emerged with no cuts and only a sprained ankle. It was the left ankle, hurt fifteen years before when she had been riding in a reckless and dangerous way a giant horse named Bucephalus. The sprain was so painful she was not able to walk. When she was X-rayed a week after the accident, no break was seen. Three weeks in a cast produced no relief, nor did several subsequent weeks in bed in traction. She gave up outside commitments and stayed in bed, secluded in the small apartment with her maid, reading and being read to by John. Early in 1927 John Marsh came home one evening with a stack of copy paper and, in effect, orders to start writing. "My God," thought Peggy, "now I've got to write a novel and what is it going to be about?"[48]

After John left for work the next day, she put on her oversized overalls and her green eyeshade (her writing outfit), put cushions for her leg under Maybelle's rickety sewing table that she used for a typing desk, stuffed the forty-five pages of 'Ropa Carmagin manuscript into a large envelope, and pushed it to one side. Then she put the stack of yellow copy paper in its place, sat down, and began to write about Scarlett O'Hara.[49]

Clearly, we have here the paradox of a writer born and reared squarely in the midst of a white racist hysteria writing a novel that very nearly omits black people as active agents in the story. Perhaps the paradox is beyond resolution, but it does seem to become less deep if we ponder the question: How black was Rhett Butler? It seems to help, too, if we think of the author as a woman who danced on the edge of her culture—sometimes in, sometimes out—and if we people who call ourselves white ask ourselves, how black are we?

Notes

1. Atlanta *Constitution,* April 14, 1899, p. 2; Atlanta *Journal,* April 15, 1899, p. 2.

2. Atlanta *Constitution,* April 24, 1899, p. 1.

3. Macon *Telegraph,* April 24, 1899, p. 1.

4. Atlanta *Journal,* April 24, 1899, pp. 1, 3; Atlanta *Constitution,* April 24, 1899, p. 2.

5. Birmingham *News,* April 24, 1899, p. 1; New York *Times,* April 25, 1899, p. 2.

6. Macon *Telegraph,* April 25, 1899, p. 6. This account of the Hose lynching draws heavily upon Lois Lineberger, "The Death of Sam Hose: A Study in the Ritual of Lynching" (Honors thesis, University of North Carolina at Chapel Hill, 1984).

7. Anne Edwards, *Road to Tara: The Life of Margaret Mitchell* (New York, 1983), 15–18; Finis Farr, *Margaret Mitchell of Atlanta: The Author of "Gone With the Wind"* (New York, 1965), 22–23. After the publication of *Gone With the Wind,* Margaret Mitchell went to extraordinary lengths to suppress literary materials (letters and manuscripts) that might provide an intimate look at her life. Indeed, she had much of this material burned. The result is that scholars have thus far not attempted to publish a "definitive" biography of Mitchell. Some of the stories told in this essay are derived from the traditions that abound concerning her life. Others are drawn from original sources. The author merely suggests that the broad themes are true, and that they merit notice.

8. Rebecca L. Felton to the Atlanta *Constitution,* December 19, 1898, clipping in Scrapbook 24, pp. 76–77, Rebecca Latimer Felton Papers, University of Georgia, Athens.

9. Joel Williamson, *The Crucible of Race,* 259–61.

10. For a general treatment of the riot, see Williamson, *Crucible,* 209–20. Historian Charles Crowe virtually rediscovered the Atlanta riot during the civil rights movement and published his findings in detail in "Racial Violence and Social Reform—Origins of the Atlanta Riot of 1906," *Journal of Negro History* 53 (July 1968): 234–56, and "Racial Massacre in Atlanta, September 22, 1906," *Journal of Negro History* 54 (April 1969): 150–75.

11. Eugene M. Mitchell to Maybelle Mitchell, September 23, 1906, Margaret Mitchell Marsh Papers, Special Collections, University of Georgia Libraries, Athens.

12. Eugene Mitchell to Maybelle Mitchell, September 25, 1906, Marsh Papers.

13. Eugene Mitchell to Maybelle Mitchell, September 29, 1906, Marsh Papers.

14. Williamson, *Crucible,* 220–23.

15. Ibid., 468–72; Eugene Mitchell to Maybelle Mitchell, September 29, 1906, Marsh Papers.

16. Edwards, *Tara,* 31–32; Margaret Mitchell to Thomas Dixon, Jr., August 5, 27, 1936, Marsh Papers, cited in *Margaret Mitchell's "Gone With the Wind" Letters, 1936–1949,* ed. Richard Harwell (New York, 1976), 52–53.

17. Williamson, *Crucible,* 140–76.

18. Edwards, *Tara,* 33, 39–41.

19. Ibid., 25–26, 42–48, 51–57; Farr, *Mitchell,* 30–31, 38.

20. Edwards, *Tara,* 57–61, 65–67; Farr, *Mitchell,* 44–45.

21. Edwards, *Tara,* 68–69, 73–75; Farr, *Mitchell,* 53–55.

22. Edwards, *Tara,* 70–71, 79–81.

23. Ibid., 70–71, 79–89; Farr, *Mitchell,* 56–57.

24. Edwards, *Tara,* 81–89, 90–92, 100–101, 107.

25. Ibid., 114–18, 125–26, 128–33; *Gone With the Wind*, 1023. All citations of *Gone With the Wind* are from the Avon edition (New York, 1973), consisting of 1024 pages.

26. *Gone With the Wind*, 564, 834.

27. Williamson, *Crucible*, 57–59.

28. *Gone With the Wind*, 646.

29. Williamson, *Crucible*, 57–59, 201–3.

30. Ralph Ellison, *Invisible Man* (New York, 1947), 364–87; Langston Hughes and Arna Bontemps, eds., *The Book of Negro Folklore* (New York, 1958), 359–63; *Gone With the Wind*, 613–14.

31. *Gone With the Wind*, 879–81, 895–99, 1021–23.

32. Ibid., 927–28.

33. Ibid., 884.

34. Ibid., 926.

35. Ibid., 310.

36. Ibid., 922–29.

37. Ibid., 931–32.

38. Ibid., 929–30.

39. Ibid., 936, 939, 944–46, 988–89, 1009, 1015, 1023.

40. Edwards, *Tara*, 128.

41. Ibid., 129–30; Farr, *Mitchell*, 76–77.

42. Edwards, *Tara*, 130.

43. William Faulkner, *Absalom, Absalom!* (New York, 1936).

44. Joseph Blotner, *Faulkner: A Biography* (New York, 1974), 358, 375.

45. Farr, *Mitchell*, 77, 103; Edwards, *Tara*, 173–74, 336 n. 129, 350.

46. Edith Hamilton, *Mythology: Timeless Tales of Gods and Heroes* (New York, 1940, 1942), 78–81.

47. As a teenage student in Atlanta's very fine Washington Seminary, Margaret took a course in mythology. Among her papers in the library of the University of Georgia in Athens, there is the notebook that she kept for the class. The notebook makes no mention of Europa, but it seems likely that Margaret knew the Europa myth. While she was not an outstanding student in the academic sense, she was certainly a close student all of her life in the things in which she was interested and about which she wrote.

48. Edwards, *Tara*, 130–32.

49. Ibid., 131–33.

The Evolution
of Heroes' Honor in the
Southern Literary Tradition

Bertram Wyatt-Brown

Among literary critics and intellectual historians there are increasing signs of a deep rethinking about the character of the Southern Renaissance. At a recent historical convention, Michael O'Brien even questioned the legitimacy of the notion "Renaissance" itself. He contends that it has been defined too narrowly and has served too long and too well the subjective purposes of Allen Tate, the critic and poet who minted the term in a famous essay fifty years ago. One can broaden the scope of the South's cultural awakening beyond Tate's boundaries so as to include sociologists, historians, and others, as Daniel Singal and Richard King have done. Yet we still run risks, O'Brien argues. The first is a tendency to identify the interwar thinkers and writers with our own political predilections, and the second, flowing from that assumption, to neglect the literary and intellectual contributions of southerners unlucky enough not to precede the Vanderbilt Agrarians and benighted enough not to share our liberal values. Although one might disagree with aspects of O'Brien's position, his questioning of long-standing premises is bold and necessary.[1]

O'Brien's commentary provides the basis for the reinterpretation that follows. Its aim, however, is limited to exactly what the title implies: the characterization of male ideals and their embodiment in the imaginative literature of the South over the centuries. (Heroines, usually better realized in women's than in men's fiction, require separate treatment.)[2] In the South, traditional male values were the chief guidelines for conduct and moral assessment—what may be called the system of honor.[3] The task of showing how southern literary history changed in relation to it cannot be fully explained in so short an essay, but we should remember at the outset how pervasive the code of honor was. It permeated both private and public circumstances, especially with regard to reputation. The community judged right and wrong, prudence and recklessness, "good" blood and "bad," shamefulness and shamelessness, the two negatives against which honor was posed and which, like honor itself, restricted individuality to knowable boundaries. A character in Lope de Vega's honor play *Los Comendadores de Córdoba* declares: "Honor is that which is contained in another; no man grants honor to himself; rather, he receives it from others." And, one might add, he must acknowledge that favorable judgment without losing dignity.[4] The old eighteenth-century notion of condescension as a virtue was based on this customarily ritualized exchange.

Honor was a lonelier business than it was ideally supposed to be. Its purpose was to strengthen ties of community, but the effect was often merely to enforce a restrictive conformity or, when carried to extremes, to satisfy obsession for power. As a result, fellowship and good cheer of a special kind were possible, but tensions between the individual and his community did arise. Feeling stained or deprived by a demeaning and unjust wrong against himself, the seeker lashes out, perhaps in murderous vengeance, because sense of selfhood and belongingness have been thrown into doubt before a watching public. Only physical violence, it is thought, can assuage the hurt and make the honor-struck man feel once more a worthy symbol of society as a whole. In Robert Penn Warren's novel *Flood,* Brad Tolliver captures this spirit when he says, "Hell, the South is the country where a man gets drunk just so he can feel lonesomer and then comes to town and picks a fight for companionship."[5] For much of its history, such costs of honor as these—and there were other ones, too—were not so readily exposed. The success of the system was based upon its universal acceptance as the only concrete, nonabstract way to conduct social affairs, and that acceptance denied the need for radical change and challenge.

From the time of earliest settlement to the Romantic period, honor was largely an unarticulated set of social expectations and rituals. Although the Chesapeake region and the Carolinas were wilderness outposts in the colonial empire, the prevailing ethic would have been familiar to the contemporary Englishman. Briefly, we should read the Augustan imitations in the southern colonies not just to find nuggets of literary beauty and craftsmanship but to understand what Tidewater squires thought important to put in representational form. Eighteenth- and nineteenth-century belles lettres served didactic more than mimetic functions: the well-worn stereotypes and stilted poses, the improbabilities of plot and happy ending had instructional purpose, and much of it was devoted to affirming old values and pieties. Given the restraints of space, Honor Experienced, as we may call the first stage, can only be illustrated by one example: the issue of preferred political style. Given the nature of planter society, it was, however, an important matter. The colonial squirearchy was basically concerned with social order, not with personal psychology or social experimentation. The gentry thought it beneath their dignity to engage in literary creativity except as part of statecraft itself. Clever satire was highly popular in eighteenth-century Virginia because class pretentiousness in a raw frontier society lent itself to absurdity. In 1761 James Reid, an indentured schoolkeeper on a plantation in King William County, gibed at the typical "Country Gentleman" who attended church "only to make bargains, hear and rehearse news, fix horse races & cock matches, and learn if there are any barbecued Hogs to be offered in sacrifice Gratis to satisfy a voracious appetite." But satirists like Reid, Robert Bolling, and Ebenezer Cooke, author of *The Sot-Weed Factor,* did not violate the code by making literary effort an end in itself. Outside the fields of social commentary, law, and political theory, intellectuality was considered effete and pretentious, a sentiment that was to hobble southern men of letters for much of southern history.[6] This was so because writing and thinking were isolating endeavors. Such activity was dangerously free of public scrutiny.

In any event, no matter how ambitious the colonial gentleman-politician might be, he was required to make his claim for power indirectly. Such circumspection served a number of functions. First, in an honor-conscious society, it demonstrated a reluctance to impose personal will on others who would otherwise suspect that the elevation of one would lower the standing of peers. Moreover, with taxation itself an affront to honor because it reduced the proprietor's material means of self-dependence, such modesty implied purity of heart: the office, no matter how lucrative, was not being sought for purposes of corrupted self-interest. Therefore the wealthiest of men were the most trustworthy, *but only so long as they did not infringe upon the rights, self-respect, and pocketbooks of their constituents,* a caveat that became increasingly difficult to sustain in the years before but most especially after the Civil War.[7]

The deferential view of political power can be located in verse—Richard Bland's poem in praise of Landon Carter, for instance.[8] But it was in drama, most especially in Robert Munford's farces *The Candidates* and *The Patriots,* that the eighteenth-century political mind found telling literary representation even though neither play was performed at the time.

Squire Munford was a traditionalist of the high aristocratic school. He believed that statesmanship should be left solely to those who could withstand the clamor of the crowd. Such men had a strong sense of place in society and a renown for Stoic prudence. The Ciceronian model later was exemplified for contemporaries in the style and repute of George Washington. Indeed, the stereotype of the gentleman as civic benefactor was part of what historians now like to call "the country-republican" ideology—that is, the American version of gentry virtue as expounded by such thinkers as Henry Bolingbroke, who eschewed court and party politics as corrupt deviations. "Men who aim at power without merit," declares the hero Meanwell in *The Patriots,* "must conceal the meanness of their souls by noisy and passionate speeches in favour of everything which is the current opinion of the day; but real patriots are mild, and secretly anxious for their country, but modest in expressions of zeal."[9]

The theme of the gentleman who stands apart from and above the mob is one that appears in later southern fiction in a manner peculiar to the South, of course, but for the pre-twentieth-century writer—the Augustan or sentimental author—such representations had direct social functions. Munford's reliance on uncomplicated, easily recognized stereotypes served to accentuate his message—indeed *was* his message: the power of True Virtue and Rightful Station over mobocracy and false, self-serving patriotism. The same links between moral and artistic purpose explain the character of the nineteenth-century romances by such writers as George Tucker, William Alexander Carruthers, and Beverley Tucker. They had to fashion new resolutions to the increasing conflicts between old wealth and new, settled habitation and frontier, ethnic diversity and Anglo-American rule, democracy and privilege, each of which had vices and virtues that threatened or promoted social and moral order in the Jacksonian South. The stereotyped "gentleman" who arose from common beginnings but was innately heroic filled the inspirational purpose that was then considered art's chief role.

After the American Revolution, writers worked out the means to incorporate the new ways with the old and to give a moral grandeur, social éclat, and Christian, even evangelical stress to the process. Yet historians and literary critics have often misunderstood the meaning of the old plantation romances. In particular, there is the misapprehension of the female role. Modern readers have assumed that men idealized the women and thereby made them irrelevant. They allegedly did so cynically to hide their mistrust of female power and capability. There was, however, no intentional deception; instead, power relationships were themselves thought of in terms of social more than individual exigencies. It was socially valuable for matrons of appropriate rank, age, and childbearing status to exercise power *within the constraints of conventional domesticity.* This was a sphere from which men were categorically excluded (the overdomesticated male was a figure of fun). If men were barred from kitchen and sewing room, women were excluded from the male world of public life. As the bearers of the families' line, plantation wives were enabled to be moral and social arbiters, deciding who was acceptable and who was not, who was marriageable and who would bring ruin. The plantation romance accepted these rigid divisions and pronounced them necessary. In particular, plantation literature was to show how slaveholders should act and what they should avoid, how readers outside the South should imagine plantation life to be and how wrong the antislavery portraits were.

Of course, imaginative writing was supposed to be entertaining as well as uplifting. The work of Poe, the humorists, and others had secular and aesthetic ends in mind. Yet, on the whole, a moral and political compass guided the antebellum plantation romancers. Their scarcely subtle themes, which exhibited strong pride in slave-state ways, were most efficiently conveyed in stereotypes and artificial plots even if the formulae make for dull modern reading.[10] From the perspective of traditional ethics, these were highly legitimate means to legitimate political ends and they well fit the plantation novelists' self-perceptions, too. By and large the romancers were gentlemen. Like their eighteenth-century predecessors and like Sir Walter Scott, their inspiration and guide, they believed that literary fame should be achieved "with the careless and negligent ease of a man of quality," as Scott phrased it. Like him, they also feared that belles lettres could "unfit us for the exercise of the useful and domestic virtues," a danger partly overcome by the moral instruction novels could pleasingly illustrate.[11]

Romance then, like romance now, offered blueprints for perfection and happiness according to the prevailing mores of the day. Those fancies were no more outrageous than the sexual heroics of Ian Fleming's adventurer. As for their fidelity to real life, one might as well criticize Busby Berkeley's lavish swim ballets as misrepresentations of 1930s depression times. Besides, in real life, too, ambiguities and irresolutions were repressed on the double grounds that God required submission to His will in a saving faith and that communal peace made such resignation imperative. Take, for instance, George Tucker's *The Valley of Shenandoah,* published in 1824. As in so many sentimental novels, the characters represent abstract principles or forces. In this case the hero, Edward Grayson, stands for the integrity of an old and lately decaying social order. Sir Walter Scott in the

Waverley series had dwelt on this theme, but it also had clear application in aristocratic Tidewater Virginia after the Revolution. James Gildon, a wealthy New Yorker, symbolizes the new commercial class that was making agrarian gentility obsolete. The sectional conflict is put into sexual terms, an allegory of honor, shame, and chastity. Gildon, though treated to the Graysons' unwise but guileless hospitality, toys with the affections of Louisa, Edward's innocent young sister. After the scoundrel's return to New York, the rejected Louisa confesses her "ruin" and Edward at once follows him. Since Gildon is Yankee and cowardly enough to reject a duel, Edward is forced to accost him in the street, only to lose his life. The passing throngs, Tucker says, are momentarily touched by the sight of this knight-errant's pale form, sensing that his actions had belonged to a nobler age. In terms of the allegorical intent, Tucker implies that the North can win by unfair means since the South is too antiquated, too pure-minded to compete with modern hedonism.

At the same time, Tucker gives redemptive powers to Edward's death. Whereas in a novel such as *Uncle Tom's Cabin* death symbolizes divine glory that even children like little Eva and blacks like Tom can share and exemplify, in this novel death is reward for purely human glory and sacrifice. Edward's letter posthumously reaches his Virginia lover Matilda Fawkner, explaining that he had been forced to pursue Gildon because "the opinion of the world" is too great for anyone to reject "its decrees of ignominy." He could not return to his betrothed or to his family "dishonoured and disgraced. That could never be." Edward vows, "I must offer you a name and a reputation on which rumour had never breathed reproach, nor suspicion left a stain. I have demanded satisfaction for the injury to my family's honour, in the only way in which it can be obtained, and I put my own life to hazard on the attempt." Tucker's didactic romance was one of the earliest plantation stories to stress the South's transcendency in the kingdom of honor, coupled with a recognition that the old ethic was no longer sacrosanct nor shared across sectional borders. Tucker approved Edward's logic about the power of reputation and the necessity of bloody "satisfaction." As a long-standing advocate of the duel (it elevated manners and forced mutual respect), he saw no ambiguities or contradictions between Christianity and revenge or between law and private justice—a perspective that Walker Percy, among others, was later to probe. Readers were expected to admire Edward, pity Louisa, rejoice at Matilda's convenient decision to join a convent, and despise Gildon, who is untouched by the law but dies "a confirmed sot."[12]

Neither Tucker nor any other southern romancer had much idea that some issues had no solution, that hierarchy of lineage or race was unjust, or that demands for chastity unfairly burdened women and left men free of restraint. Such thoughts would have thrown into question the whole moral order as sanctified by Holy Writ and Anglo-American tradition. Self-repression (then called self-discipline) was a prime social virtue; one did what others thought right and honorable, not what the heart or other parts of the anatomy prompted. As Louis Rubin has observed, outward appearances counted most and deep introspections least. Nineteenth-century southern literature reflected these priorities.[13] Thus, a major function of the southern sentimental novel was to confirm, celebrate, and elaborate upon the uses of honor through the heroics of some and the villainy of others. But it was more than that, too, according to the "reader-response" approach of Jane Tompkins. The point that William Gilmore Simms had in mind, for instance, was to illustrate in his historical novels how southern whites had evolved from primitive to refined forms of social behavior and would continue to do so. In some plantation romances we find almost consciously realized tensions and hints of doubt about the rightness and justice of things, ones that Anne Jones is particularly sensitive in explicating. But her insights were not available to the readers of that day because anomalies and antinomies were not culturally relevant to their experiences. They interpreted texts in the light of conventions totally alien to us. As Michael Kreyling says, "A social, cultural group accepts its narrative form, and rejects others, because that form alone embodies the group's nearest image of itself in its most truthful and accessible scripture."[14]

The whole thrust of the romance was directed toward shoring up the long-revered values that had been the justification for resolute action in secession, war, and Redemption. For another generation it was still possible to maintain a communion of memory. In literature, Thomas Nelson Page, John Esten Cooke, and others provided the bread and wine of that ritual. Remembering together—in storytelling, monument unveiling, veteran parading—was a collective way to deny that all the sacrifice and ruin had been a perverse, monstrous waste.

The result, of course, was derivative fare because its value for contemporaries lay in its immediate familiarity, its expression of the region's social and public norms, not its transcendence over them. Quoting Yeats, James McBride Dabbs of South Carolina lamented that in antebellum times the slave states produced "neither poets nor saints," at least not ones capable of making substantial "the soul of their people." The Old South *"never really quarreled with itself"* and grew "adept" merely "at quarreling with others," for which "the instruments of rhetoric and eloquence," not imaginative literature and poetry, were sufficient. He was right, but we should remember that novelists then had instructional, not purely aesthetic, aims.[15]

The southern artist was necessarily unadventurous. There was no cultural or social basis upon which modern concepts of literature could rest. Who had the nerve or intuition for challenging communal tradition, making ruthless use of neighbors, relatives and well-known local incidents as the soil from which to grow individualized characters and situations? Certainly the dilemma of the highly gifted diarist Mary Chesnut arose from the fact that she could not afford to risk reputation in Camden where there was no friend like Faulkner's Phil Stone, no clique of rebellious literati to stimulate, criticize, and support her. Despite her many gifts, she could neither publish her critical, penetrating journals as they were nor translate them into a fictional mode. It was not slavery that hobbled her literary self-confidence. Greece, Rome, Russia, and other civilizations managed rather well to produce enduring literature despite, or perhaps because of, coerced labor arrangements. Rather, it was the southern community with its hobbling provinciality, its sense of inferiority, its suspicion of intellect, and its destructive gossip and intrusions that stood in the path. Such attitudes stifled experimentation: it was best to follow the old formulae for plot, style, and characterization. Nineteenth-century southerners did not really wish to understand psychological tensions, ironies, and thick social complications. Local-color sketches amused; heavy matters did not. Life was hard enough as it was.[16]

Only a few southern writers started to find a different role for the artist, one appropriate to a more pluralistic, secular, and institutional society: Mark Twain, Kate Chopin, George W. Cable toward the close of the long romantic era. Turn-of-the-century critics, drunk on New South rhetoric, proclaimed—just as 1860 secessionists had done before them—the dawning of a literary Renaissance. But these academic prophets could not free themselves from the past—most especially from the drama of "decimated families, smoking homesteads, and the passing forever of a civilization unique in human history," as C. Alphonso Smith put it in 1898. "*But*," he continued, "*literature loves a lost cause, provided honor be not lost*." Although northern authors like Henry James had more sophisticated aims in mind, Smith and other southern contemporaries still had no reason to question, probe, or reflect.[17]

When that flowering of literature, so long heralded, actually did appear in the 1920s, it took a form of which Alphonso Smith and most others would have disapproved. At last the South had reached the point when searching commentary upon the dying code was possible. Interestingly, honor, in both its domestic and its public forms, was the chief literary target of the Faulkner generation. If it had been southern Protestantism and prudery, then why is anticlericalism and explicit sex so absent from central concern? Instead the writers were preoccupied with the distances between what the grandfathers had asserted and the fathers had repeated to them so irresolutely. (Richard King, the intellectual historian, has recently explained the matter well.) In 1947 James Branch Cabell recalled how as a youngster before World War I he had noticed the ritual ways in which his elders addressed "woman hood . . . the brightness of hope's rainbow . . . the scroll of fame . . . the verdict of posterity" and the "thin line of heroes who had warred for righteousness' sake in vane." He understood that it was all done without conscious hypocrisy or prevarication. Gentlemen did "not tell lies," but, Cabell noted, they could be reticent about uncomfortable truths. It was amazing, he wrote, that in ordinary talk, in a different setting among close friends, these public mythologizers whispered, for instance, that some "Confederate Arthuriad" had not uttered a soldierly last word but had called for the bedpan. The "half-mythopoeic and half-critical frame of mind" that the older folks found congenial has always been the traditional style, but it had become almost unintelligible to those like Cabell unable to share the old assumptions.[18]

What was so impressive about the post—World War I generation's creativity was not the rise of an intellectual self-confidence capable of breaking the cake of custom, but the writers' struggle with it. Regret mingled with hope, dismay with admiration. The ethic of the Old Order was reexamined in order to provide an angle of moral vision never before attempted in the South. Take, for example, Allen Tate's poem "The Meaning of Life," a reflection on his childhood in Kentucky:

> The old men shot at one another for luck;
> It made me think I was like none of them.
> At twelve I was determined to shoot only
> For honor; at twenty not to shoot at all;
> I know at thirty-three that one must shoot
> As often as one gets the rare chance—
> In killing there is more than commentary.

As Robert Dupree explains, Tate means here that one must take responsibility for one's actions, that shooting, as ritual behavior, was a way of finding order in life.[19] Honor to the twelve-year-old was a superficial principle, as it was for all too many antebellum southerners with their duels and street brawls, but as an adult the poet comes to see that circumstances may arise when one must choose. The concern is with individuality, selfhood; old honor was largely a public, social, collective matter.

Most remarkable of all, of course, was Faulkner's understanding of the code and its destructive as well as inspiring features. Although Faulkner did not subscribe to the ethic, he remained fascinated with how people acted in accordance with it—consciously and otherwise—and how these actions and convictions gave purpose and spirit to the Old South. He knew that behind the postwar myths lay a coherent if crude mode of organizing social life. Take Thomas Sutpen, for instance, who Faulkner shows based his life upon the outward appearances of honor and regard, though he never understood its other component—the expectation of reciprocity. The man who claims esteem must give it, too, because those who offer esteem have a dignity of their own that must be acknowledged. William Hazlitt, the early nineteenth-century English essayist, wisely noted that "a gentleman is one who understands and shows every mark of deference to the claims of self love in others and exacts it in return from them." That is the significance of Sutpen's death at the hands of Wash Jones. Even the worthless poor white could feel violated and could react in hatred and contempt. Sutpen's weakness, his vulnerability, or what General Compson calls his "innocence," lay in his misapprehension of what the code required: open expression of mutual respect, a complex value that involves love as well as fear, intimacy as well as distance, even across the lines of hierarchy itself. In different and obsessive ways, Rosa Millard, John Sartoris, Gail Hightower, and Lucas Beauchamp, to name a few in Faulkner's world, were victims of honor, in their own actions or in those of others, even as each in separate ways represented its glory, too.[20]

But others in the interwar period took honor as seriously as Faulkner. For instance, Caroline Gordon also counterposes nostalgia with hard-eyed objectivity. *Penhally* (1931), her first novel, explores the decline of honor through one Kentucky family.[21] Nicholas Llewellyn, the central figure, acts on the basis of a conservative tradition that Robert Munford of colonial Virginia would have applauded. Nick believes so strongly in his family headship as eldest brother and in the already obsolete custom of entailment that he refuses to divide the parental estate with Ralph, his younger brother, and permits no reconciliation when Ralph moves off the old estate to establish his own independence.

Like one of Munford's heroes, Nick stays aloof from the secession clamor around him. He waits out the war, buying not Confederate bonds but gold so that Penhally survives the disaster. In contrast, Ralph, a romantic soul, sacrifices his fortune for the Confederacy and dies at the close of the conflict, hallucinating about the noble southern cause. But if eighteenth-century Honor Experienced triumphs in Nick's shrewd policies and antebellum honor, transformed and romanticized, fails in Ralph's destruction, the story is not didactic. Caroline Gordon recognized that the old order based on freedom from alien constraints and raw personal will was as corrupt in its way as the modern ideology of money which replaced it. Nick is admirable, but his obsession with power and abstract principle and his daunting compulsion to hate help to account for the later generation's tragedy of emotional ruin and fratricide. One is reminded of *Absalom, Absalom!* in the claustrophobic intensity of family life that Gordon portrays here, but the novel, though underrated, seems oddly reminiscent of the static characterizations in the old romances, as if there was some hidden chasm between the modern genre and the authorial intent. For all the faults in realization, however, Gordon has artfully created a believable patriarch in Nicholas Llewellyn. His sense of honor is complex: he is both cruelly intransigent in self-defense and effective and awesome in protecting those for whom he is responsible. He was a man, she implies, with ideals worth living and dying for, whereas the modern southerner, indeed the modern American, has no such dream, no such grandeur.[22]

In different form, this theme is present in the work of Walker Percy, too: the solidity of the old ideals, the barrenness of the present. But unlike Faulkner or Gordon, Percy, one of the last of this literary era, claims a chief concern with loss of memory rather than with explorations of the past or its impositions upon the present.[23] His heroes are likely to suffer more from amnesia than from obsession with ancient woes. Whereas Warren's Jack Burden and Faulkner's Quentin Compson search for meaning by ventures into family history, Percy's heroes have almost no genuine intimacy with others, not even with ghosts, although most do end up with another companion of the spirit. Deprecating an overconcern with southern legend and history, Percy argues that his heroes all "find themselves in a here-and-now predicament."[24]

Those dilemmas, however, are by no means divorced from the past—including the Percy family heritage of honor, suicide, and melancholy—nor from the old ethic and memories of its former strength in the South. The very names of the characters, with their chivalric and southern resonances, belie the point to some degree. In a revealing analogy, Percy told an interviewer, "In a way, Binx Bolling [in *The Moviegoer*] is Quentin Compson who didn't commit suicide." In *Lancelot* more than in earlier and somewhat more optimistic novels, Percy deals with madness and male honor in a most anguished and tragic fashion—a violence that involves the murder of others rather than with self-killing. Lancelot is fully aware of his lineage: he tells Father John, his "confessor" and childhood friend, that he belonged to "an honorable family with an honorable name." But, like Warren's Judge Irwin, Lancelot's father hid corruption behind the mask of rectitude. Commenting on the discovery, Lancelot says, "If there is one thing harder to bear than dishonor, it is honor, being brought up in a family where everything is so nice, perfect in fact, except of course oneself."[25]

In this, Percy's most chilling novel, Lancelot's ideological enemies are both Christian faith and modern secularism.[26] His fury comes out in murderous vengeance under the rubric of a Stoic, fatalistic honor: a vindication against cuckoldry, against the adultery of a "liberated" wife, symbolizing a culture that no longer understands either shame or sin. Whereas Tucker's Grayson acts out of loyalty to family in his pathetically fumbled revenge, Percy's Lancelot exploits honor to mask his own emptiness and, one suspects, self-despising. Yet he tries to find larger purpose. In his insanity, which actually mirrors the degeneracy of those against whom he raves, Lancelot fancies a "New Reformation" where he can start again "in the Wilderness where Lee lost." Since love is impossible in this world anyhow, "there will be tight-lipped courtesy between men. And chivalry toward women. . . . Women will once again be strong and modest." And children will be happy because they know "what they are to do." Yet, as Percy makes clear, Lancelot is no less implicated in evil than those betrayers of his trust against whom he rages. "Dishonor," Lancelot says perversely, "is sweeter and more mysterious than honor. It holds a secret. There is no secret in honor."[27] Clearly the moral ambiguity of antique honor which made a virtue of murder for the sake of family pride finds expression here in a way closed to a writer like Thomas Dixon, who lived when southern convention *required* an intimate connection between honor and white female purity.

In fact, Percy's theme and rendering of Lancelot's psychology has more European than southern allusions. First, there are the Quixotic resonances: after all, we remember, Cervantes' melancholic knight took as his ideal the lusty, maddened Arthurian Launcelot du Lac, not the pious Sir Percivale or Galahad. Second, one observes that Percy's *Lancelot* uncannily resembles the machinery of Spanish Golden Age honor plays. It may be likened to Calderón's bleakly existential *A Secreto Agravio, Secreta Venganza (Secret Vengeance for Secret Insult)*. Calderón, like Percy and like Shakespeare in *Othello,* makes the point that honor, when carried out to the letter, distorts and dehumanizes rather than ennobles. This is so because such an injury to the ego as sexual betrayal exists more in the mind of the wounded party than in public awareness, a situation which prompts the often devious means used to gain incriminating proof. Using heat-sensitive video cameras, Lancelot sees distorted shapes of lovers, shadows representing the confusions of his mind. As in the case of Calderón's Lope, the inner turmoil which produces the suspicions stems from already existing self-doubts about career and even virility. These melancholic heroes react by practically throwing their wives at men to whom the women are attracted, yet blame the allegedly weaker sex, not themselves, and plan elaborate means of detecting the wrong, half hoping to prove themselves cuckolded to justify their unmanageable fury and depression. "Oh," cries Calderón's Don Lope, whose suspicions of his wife become self-fulfilling, "the world's insane legalities! That a man who has ever labored in the cause of honor cannot know if he has been insulted!" Percy intends us to recall the age-old traditions of that self-vindication which must bend to "blind custom's cudgelings," as Calderón's Don Lope complains. Its existence, particularly in Mediterranean culture and life, is highlighted in *Lancelot* by the repetition of an earlier killing. During one encounter with his friend, Lancelot tells the story of an ancestor, a planter of Natchez in Spanish-held Louisiana. The "Don" slits the throat of a defeated and angry gambler in an informal duel with a bowie knife, the southern frontiersman's "broadsword," for the offense of traducing his mother's name. Lancelot slays his wife's lover in conscious imitation of that great-grandsire, using the same weapon upon the same part of the anatomy and for the same reason, the perceived affront to manhood through an insult upon a woman for whom he held himself accountable.[28]

Yet, denying the influence of the past, a repudiation which his actions disprove, Lancelot also denies that the discovered adultery aroused his anger or shame; it caused him only "a prickling at the base of the spine, a turning of the worm of interest." We are not to believe his dispassionateness. Certainly, under similar circumstances, Faulkner never expected us to believe that Thomas Sutpen felt no deep disgrace when, as a poor-white Virginia youngster, a slave house servant rebuffed him at a Tidewater planter's door. The incident, like Lancelot's reaction to Margot's deception, was the basis of Sutpen's prideful design. Honor could be internalized and might even lead to personal fulfillment. Yet, as in the portrayals of Lancelot and Sutpen, avoidance of self-knowledge was all too common. Reflection inhibited action; repression prompted it. What Lancelot felt—were he capable of feeling—was humiliation and his response was to avenge it, a psychology not of conscience but of honor. He says, "I know what a trespass or an injury or an insult is—something to be set right."[29]

Yet sin and guilt are not burned into this cavalier's heart any more than in Don Lope's. In both works we are made aware of the heroes' wrongdoing by observing the action through their eyes, a solipsistic perspective. No less schizophrenic than Lancelot, Don Lope wreaks vengeance on both parties. He kills his wife and burns the house where she lies dead, and he drowns her lover. Like Lancelot, Lope survives and remains unpunished by the law. The king accepts the nobleman's rationale: "secret insult most requires secret vengeance," words applicable to Lancelot as well. The difference in their characters is that Lope seems at the end to have a tinge of regret for his passion and crime, whereas Lancelot has none. For both Calderón's seventeenth-century audience and Percy's present-day one, the heroes are hollow shells, driven by "principles" that mask the inner emptiness. The ancient and the modern lesson is simple: the vindicator may save his honor but lose his soul.[30]

In the context of his role as a transitional figure in this evolutionary scheme, Percy's connection with the writer John Kennedy Toole was most appropriate. The senior novelist helped to see the young deceased author's *A Confederacy of Dunces* published in 1980. In this great farce, honor becomes, as it does for a number of contemporary writers, abused or forgotten. The ethic is a subject of nihilistic laughter—but with the customary underlying moral criticism which has always been satire's function. More accurately, we should call it a Swiftian "reverse satire" in which Ignatius J. Reilly, the hero (like Percy's Lancelot), is as guilty of venality as is the consumer society of which Reilly is a bloated, hot-dog-gorging example. Although Toole's character is no gentleman and the supporting cast consists of New Orleans lowlifers or nouveaux riches, the philosophy around which the book is centered is that of the Christian Stoic Boethius. Like Percy, who brought his book to light, the author is ambivalent about Stoicism. Reilly's wild intemperateness and his refusal to accept life's vagaries are as far from Boethius's advice as one can get. If Faulkner read Cervantes every year, as we are told he did, Toole, in the flatulent form of Reilly, actually becomes a modern-day Don Quixote. In surrealistic style, he organizes a New Orleans Sodomites' peace movement to Save the World Through Degeneracy and plunges into a crusade for "Moorish dignity" at the pants factory where he works. But the quest is neither for a "Holy Grail" nor an "unholy" one, in the manner of

Percy's cynic-idealist Lancelot.[31] Reilly's spluttering horror of the New South's work ethic and his Miniver Cheevylike medievalism mock the old New Orleanian claim for leisure and noblesse.

In this fantasy of shamelessness, as it were, the Night of Joy bar in the French Quarter becomes a crazy modern replication of the old plantation. When Lana Lee, muscle-bottomed proprietress, leaves on a shopping trip, Jones, her newly hired black sweeper, says: "Wha she go shoppin for? A whip?"[32] Promoted to street barker, Jones shouts to the passing public: "Night of Joy got genuine color peoples workin below the minimal wage. Whoa! Guarantee plantation atmosphere, got cotton growin right on the stage . . . got a civil right worker gettin his ass beat up between show. Hey!" The chief attraction at Night of Joy is Darlene, a very dumb stripper with a weirdly trained cockatoo. Vainly Lana Lee tries to improve Darlene's gig by rehearsing her for the role of Harlett O'Hara, an Old South belle in crinoline and big hat. Harla O'Horror, as the barker Jones calls her, is supposed to have just attended a ball where, Lana Lee says indelicately,

> "a lot of southern gentlemen were trying to feel you up over the fried chicken and hog jowls. But you cooled them all. Why? Because you're a lady dammit. You come onstage . . . . You got your little pet [bird] with you . . . and you say to it, 'There was plenty of beaux at that ball, honey, but I still got my honor.' Then the goddam bird starts grabbing at your dress. You're shocked, you're surprised, you're innocent. But you're too refined to stop it. Got it?"

The actual performance is one of the zaniest scenes in southern literature. So much for the plantation legend and W. J. Cash's lily-pure Arthurian Maid of Astolat.[33]

Toole understood the southern eccentric, and Reilly's pretensions, though flamboyantly larger than life, have analogs in the lonely lives that southern life sometimes created. In his evident despair, which is always an aspect of mock-heroes, Reilly brings to mind, for instance, so neurotic a figure as John Randolph of Bizarre. Randolph's classical erudition, sexual inadequacies, and choleric temper resemble Reilly's, however different their girth, class, and political importance. More typically crankish than Randolph are those oddballs to be found deed-searching for corporations in the county courthouses of the Lower South or teaching English literature or Romance languages at the local academy or country college. Usually they are unmarried and often live with their mothers or with dusty memories of them. They rail against Yankees and modernity, claiming that civilization ended when Louis XVI lost his head. We all know the

122

type. Their tattered monarchism is harmless because it mirrors the conservatism still abroad in the region. But the breed is dying out.

Although *A Confederacy of Dunces* was written in the early 1960s, its spirit really belongs to the 1970s. No longer was honor regretted or even cursed. Like Toole's, the contemporary novelist Harry Crews's intention is to show through the medium of the grotesque the moral anemia of a South stripped of tradition and meaning. In his novel *Karate Is a Thing of the Spirit,* published in 1972, for instance, one finds parallels with Toole's picaresque.[34] In both *Karate* and *Dunces,* the sexual lines are blurred, as if the ruination of the old ethic of male honor has promoted the sexual ambiguities of the modern world. John Kaimon, the young hero, later becomes highly virile with a blonde karateka and beauty queen. At the start, however, he is a lost androgynous soul, a kind of male Temple Drake, raped by a motorcycle gang and two transvestites who catch him when both his hands are in heavy casts from the training exercise of bludgeoning concrete in a dry swimming pool. Also Crews, like Toole, deals with transients and lowlifers, not the distracted gentlemen-heroes who inhabit the world of Walker Percy or William Styron. Crews's hero appropriately bears the name of the American crocodile, the caiman.

Whereas Styron and Percy see some hope to be salvaged from the older tradition, Crews, like Toole, projects a nihilistic outcome, an absence of faith in anything including literature itself. The Southern Renaissance writers themselves become fit subjects of latter-day ribaldry. They serve as icons of irrelevance, commentaries on the sterility of the past as a means for present-day self-authentification. John Kaimon wears a William Faulkner T-shirt, a symbol that the southern literary tradition has as much meaning as those Confederate decals of an angry coot saying, "Hell, no, I'll never forget." Kaimon justifies his choice of apparel on the grounds of loyalty to his hometown of Oxford, but he did not even go to "Ole Miss" to study literature. He just went to the Oxford high school. The plot, set on the "Sun 'n Fun" beaches of South Florida, concerns Kaimon's involvement in a karate group. This commune of the obsessed is a far cry from the old-fashioned kin and neighbor spirit of which southerners boast. The guru of the muscled fanatics is a midget named Jefferson Davis Munroe, an unlikely tag that conjures up the names of three southern-born presidents. Munroe's followers "admired and loved him" but they "could not help their shame." In sympathy, the hero says, "Well . . . if he meets another midget, he can sure whip *his* ass."[35]

Like *A Confederacy of Dunces,* the Crews novel, in appropriate Old Festival comedy style, ends in bacchanalia and escape "to the green woods," a form found in ancient Greek plays and Shakespeare's *As You Like It,* and revived in E. M. Forster's *Passage to India* and *Maurice*—all of them rather androgynous in character. The portrait of the South that comes through this work, however, more nearly resembles Ken Kesey's California of the Altamont era than it does Mardi Gras New Orleans. Neither the rituals of southern religion nor those of southern honor, Crews seems to say, can any longer support community life or personal growth—either in the region or in the nation at large. Crews's world of ritual chops and oriental screams is the antithesis of Old South courtesy which is so insignificant that it finds no manifestation even in derision here. It is simply forgotten. Instead, the rites of an older day when women stood on their isolated pedestals are enacted in the form of glittery beauty contests run by a mobile-home entrepreneur. Meaning and redemption cannot be found in these things, Crews implies. The self-discipline but essential materialism of karate also proves an insufficient anchor. In a microbus, the hero runs away into a meaningless sunset with his pageant queen of violence and orgasm.[36]

Karate is not a lone phenomenon. Take Barry Hannah's novella *Ray,* for instance. The hero, an alcoholic Tuscaloosa physician with a fourth-rate practice and a penchant for violence, is as promiscuously alive as Quentin Compson is impotent and suicidal. The thrust of Hannah's novel is directed not against honor, which becomes a subject of wild parody, but against southern Jesus Saves religion, a topic not so often pilloried by those of Faulkner's generation. Instead, Hannah's *Ray* reminds us of Philip Roth's *Portnoy's Complaint* because of the explicit sexuality of the hero's rebellion. The villain of the story is the Reverend Maynard Castro who murders the hero's mistress, a country rock singer. Preachers, says Ray derisively, "seem benevolent, but they are more evil than the rest of us walking the pavement." Hannah seems much angrier at religion than his predecessors were. "I like generally the kind of people that blow the mind of the middle class," he told an interviewer. That kind of attitude and tone cannot be called "old southern." Yet strong traces of the region's literary tradition are quite evident, especially elements from Flannery O'Connor's *Wise Blood,* Percy's *Love in the Ruins,* and Crews's *The Gospel Singer,* in which Willalee Bookatee Hull, a black disciple of a revivalist, murders his first convert.[37]

Hannah may consider himself free of the preoccupations with history and tradition that had gripped his literary predecessors in the South, but he too takes some swipes at the old ethic. Throughout the book, as if to mock Chick Mallison's famous musings about Civil War glories in *Intruder in the Dust,* Ray fantasizes an encounter with Jeb Stuart at Gettysburg, with dialogue out of a Hollywood plantation film, rated R. But the Vietnam war, not the "Bloody Chasm," as Gerald Johnson once called it, is Ray's experience.[38]

The other method of dealing with the past is to ignore it rather than demean it. Turning to a new arrival on the southern literary scene, we find in Padgett Powell an author with almost no referents to southern history. Although less satiric and much less low-class in character portrayals than Crews, Powell's brilliant first novel *Edisto* is set on the Sea Islands of South Carolina. In part the story concerns the economic and social upheaval there which has washed in a tide of Arabian millionaires and country-club types to play in the sun. Simons Everson Manigault, the oddly precocious boy-hero of this *bildungsroman* or apprenticeship novel, belongs to an old plantation family, but nobody seems calcified by memories of ancient glories. The sole reference to the Old South comes early in the novel when Simons remarks:

> Because when your Southern barony is reduced as ours is to a tract of clay roads cut in a feathery herbaceous jungle of deerfly for stock and scrub oak for crop, and the great house is a model beach house resembling a pagoda, and the planter's wife is abandoned by the planter, as ours has been, and she has only one servant left . . . well, that vestigial baroness insists that vestigial slave do her one duty right—"the linen"—all that remains of cotton finery.

The book is clearly southern, with some subtle reshapings of old miscegenationist themes in the characters of Taurus and Theenie.[39] The problems are nonetheless largely present-minded in a way that Walker Percy preached but shrewdly did not wholly practice. The blacks in the story act in a natural way—undefensive, bemused by white antics, and likable simply as people. Careful reading of the work will reveal more ingenuity than we can explore here. But Powell does represent a shift in literary focus away from the past. With this change there has come an acceptance of the South on its own terms, a comfortableness, even complacency, about being southern. It is as though Shreve McCannon asks no more questions and Quentin Compson, leaving his watch untouched, reaches the conclusion that it does not matter if he hates or loves his homeland.

Quite unmistakably, the theme of honor has run its course. The grasp of history and memory has been forever relinquished, as Lewis Simpson reminds us in *The Dispossessed Garden*.[40] What the trends are seems clear. The classic themes of tension between a well-defined but decadent ethical system and a shiny, corrupt, and flabby modern one have dissolved. The artist's quarrel with existential problems of the American rather than purely southern contemporary scene has replaced them. To be sure, southern novelists today are exploring the dislocating effects of vast change upon the region. No doubt they will continue to do so. But the breakdown of a rural order in the face of urban modernity is hardly something unique; immigrants and folk from other parts of an older America have experienced these things and their dilemmas have found literary expression.

In looking back along the continuum, we cannot doubt that the most moving literature in the South was produced when honor was revealed and its passing regretted. Michael O'Brien is right to call for a relabeling of the "Renaissance." Like an old tire, its tread is worn from overuse, a common fate of historical terms. Yet, whatever may be the choice to rechristen that brief moment in American literary history, who could deny the specialness of those interwar writers? They understood their forefathers' profound and ancient legacy in a way denied us now. They could not help but grieve its passing from America. Looking forward, one can say that whatever contemporary southern writers will achieve, their inventiveness no longer depends upon the relationship of the southern past to present circumstances. For better or worse, the sands of that hourglass have run out.

Notes

1. Michael O'Brien, "Historical Perspectives on the Southern Renaissance" (Paper presented at the Organization of American Historians meeting in Los Angeles, April 7, 1984, to be published in an essay collection on southern topics under the editorship of James Cobb). On historiographical neglect of women writers, see Anne Goodwyn Jones, "Faulkner's Daughters: Women of the Southern Literary Renaissance" (Paper presented at the OAH meeting in Los Angeles, April 7, 1984). See also Daniel J. Singal, *The War Within: From Victorian to Modernist Thought in the South, 1919–1945* (Chapel Hill, 1982); Richard H. King, "Victorian to Modernist Thought," *Southern Literary Journal* 15 (Spring 1983): 127; C. Vann Woodward, "Why the Southern Renaissance?" *Virginia Quarterly Review* 51 (Spring 1975): 227–29; and Michael O'Brien, *The Idea of the American South, 1920–1941* (Baltimore, 1979), especially pp. xi–xvii, 3–27.

2. Because of the limitations of space, I have not tried to include women and black writers or to explore very fully the issues of gender and race that a long and comprehensive monograph would allow.

3. See Bertram Wyatt-Brown, *Southern Honor: Ethics and Behavior in the Old South* (New York, 1982), and *Yankee Saints and Southern Sinners* (Baton Rouge, 1985).

4. Lope de Vega, *Los Comendadores de Córdoba*, quoted in Donald R. Larson, *The Honor Plays of Lope de Vega* (Cambridge, Mass., 1977), 5. Upon retirement in 1828, Senator John Randolph of Virginia voiced this concept when he exclaimed, "I shall receive from [my loyal constituents] the only reward I ever looked for, but the highest men can receive—the universal expression of their approbation." See Henry Adams, *John Randolph* (New York, 1961 [1882]), 193. For an ethnic American view of honor (*rispetto*) and shame (*vergogna*), see Robert Anthony Orsi, *The Madonna of 115th Street: Faith and Community in Italian Harlem, 1880–1950* (New Haven, 1985), especially pp. 107–49.

5. Warren quoted in Lewis P. Simpson, *The Dispossessed Garden: Pastoral and History in Southern Literature* (Athens, Ga., 1975), 92.

6. Robert D. Arner, "Literature in the Eighteenth-Century Colonial South," in Louis D. Rubin, Jr., ed., *The History of Southern Literature* (Baton Rouge, 1985), 40–42; Drew Faust, *A Sacred Circle: The Dilemma of the Intellectual in the Old South, 1840–1860* (Baltimore, 1977); and Faust, *James Henry Hammond and the Old South: A Design for Mastery* (Baton Rouge, 1982).

7. See J. Mills Thornton III, *Politics and Power in a Slave Society: Alabama, 1800–1860* (Baton Rouge, 1978), 100–105.

8. Richard Bland, "An Epistle to Landon Carter, Esq., Upon Hearing that He does not intend to Stand a Candidate at the Next Election of Burgesses," in Louis D. Rubin, Jr., *The Literary South* (New York, 1979), 51–53, quotations 52. Thomas Burke, an Eastern Shore Virginian, took a more jaundiced view of Carter some years later, and in his poem called "Transmogrification," with classical references, claimed the gods had magically changed "Carter into an Ass." See Thomas Burke, "Transmogrification," in Rubin, *Literary South*, 53–54.

9. See Courtlandt Canby, ed., "Robert Munford's *The Patriots*," *William and Mary Quarterly*, 3d ser., 6 (July 1949): 437–503. "His political notions," says Meanwell of Brazen, a "violent patriot" who "understands little or nothing beyond a dice-box and race-field, but thinks he knows every thing; and woe be to him that contradicts him" (p. 449). See also Jay B. Hubbell and Douglass Adair, eds., "Robert Munford's *The Candidates*," *William and Mary Quarterly*, 3d ser., 5 (April 1948): 217–57; Lewis Leary, "1776–1815," in Rubin, *History of Southern Literature*, 69–70.

10. Mary Ann Wimsatt, "Antebellum Fiction," in Rubin, *History of Southern Literature*, 92–107.

11. Anne Firor Scott, *The Southern Lady: From Pedestal to Politics, 1830–1930* (Chicago, 1970); Anne Goodwyn Jones, *Tomorrow Is Another Day: The Woman Writer in the South, 1859–1936* (Baton Rouge, 1981), 51–95; William R. Taylor, *Cavalier and Yankee: The Old South and American National Character* (New York, 1963 [1961]). Scott quoted in Robert C. Gordon, *Under Which King: A Study of the Scottish Waverley Novels* (New York, 1969), 1, 3. Scott was instrumental in transforming honor from its clannish base to a more selfless and thoroughly English version, so much so that sacrifice of love in favor

of high-minded abstinence and sense of duty becomes associated with honor in its Victorian formulation. See also Robert C. Gordon, "Scott, Racine, and the Future of Honor," in J. H. Alexander and David Hewitt, eds., *Scott and His Influence: The Papers of the Aberdeen Scott Conference, 1982* (Aberdeen, 1983), 260.

12. George Tucker, *The Valley of Shenandoah or Memoirs of the Graysons*, 2 vols. (Chapel Hill, 1970 [1824]), II, 305–6 (quotations). Cf. Ritchie Devon Watson, Jr., *The Cavalier in Virginia Fiction* (Baton Rouge, 1985), 71–79. See also George Tucker, "On Duelling," in *Essays on Various Subjects of Taste, Morals and National Policy* (Georgetown, 1822), 250–59, and Jane Tompkins, *Sensational Designs: The Cultural Work of American Fiction, 1790–1860* (New York, 1985), especially her chapter on *Uncle Tom's Cabin*, 122–46.

13. Louis D. Rubin, Jr., *William Elliott Shoots a Bear* (Baton Rouge, 1975), 27.

14. Mary Ann Wimsatt, "Realism and Romance in Simms's Midcentury Fiction," *Southern Literary Journal* 12 (Spring 1980): 29–48; John C. Guilds, "Simms's Use of History: Theory and Practice," *Mississippi Quarterly* 30 (Fall 1977): 505–11. See also Tompkins, *Sensational Designs*, xii–xix; Michael Kreyling, "The Hero in Antebellum Southern Narrative," *Southern Literary Journal* 16 (Spring 1984): 5; and Kreyling, *Figures of the Hero in Southern Narrative* (Baton Rouge, 1987), 9–29.

15. Dabbs quoted by Walker Percy, "Random Thoughts on Southern Literature, Southern Politics, and the American Future," *Georgia Review* 32 (Fall 1978): 507–8.

16. Susan Snell, "Phil Stone of Yoknapatawpha" (MS under preparation for publication, kindly lent by author); C. Vann Woodward, ed., *Mary Chesnut's Civil War* (New Haven, 1981), xv–liii.

17. Lucinda Hardwick MacKethan, *The Dream of Arcady: Place and Time in Southern Literature* (Baton Rouge, 1980), 41; J. V. Ridgely, *Nineteenth-Century Southern Literature* (Lexington, 1980), 99–111, 116 (quotation).

18. James Branch Cabell, *Let Me Lie: Being in the Main an Ethnological Account of the Remarkable Commonwealth of Virginia and the Making of Its History* (New York, 1947), 145, 154, 155, 159.

19. See Robert S. Dupree, *Allen Tate and the Augustinian Imagination: A Study of the Poetry* (Baton Rouge, 1983), 149.

20. William Faulkner's perspective on honor is expertly revealed in Warwick Wadlington, *Reading Faulknerian Tragedy* (Ithaca, 1987). Hazlitt quoted in Shirley Robin Letwin, *The Gentleman in Trollope: Individuality and Moral Conduct* (Cambridge, Mass., 1982), 15. Lynn Levins and others erroneously interpret the Old South's constructions of gentility and honor as mere delusion and not functional ideal. Cf. Lynn Gartrell Levins, *Faulkner's Heroic Design: The Yoknapatawpha Novels* (Athens, Ga., 1976), 119. See also William Faulkner to Malcolm Cowley, [early November 1944], in Malcolm Cowley, *The Faulkner-Cowley File: Letters and Memories, 1944–1962* (New York, 1978), 15.

21. On Caroline Gordon's devotion to her southern heritage, see Robert H. Brinkmeyer, Jr., *Three Catholic Writers of the Modern South* (Jackson, Miss., 1985), 79.

22. On Nick's honorable sensibility in shooting the lecherous Yankee, see Rose Ann C. Fraistat, *Caroline Gordon as Novelist and Woman of Letters* (Baton Rouge, 1984), 57.

23. Panthea Reid Broughton, "Gentlemen and Fornicators: *The Last Gentleman* and a Bisected Reality," in Broughton, ed., *The Art of Walker Percy: Stratagems for Being* (Baton Rouge, 1979), 98–99.

24. Lewis A. Lawson, "The Fall of the House of Lamar," in Broughton, *The Art of Walker Percy*, 219–20. Percy quotations from Jo Gulledge, "The Reentry Option: An Interview with Walker Percy," *Southern Review*, n.s., 20 (January 1984): 106. On suicide, see William Rodney Allen, "All the Names of Death: Walker Percy and Hemingway," *Mississippi Quarterly* 36 (Winter 1982–83): 3–19.

25. Walker Percy, *Lancelot* (New York, 1977), 41, 42; Gulledge, "The Reentry Option," 107.

26. Percy, *Lancelot*, 177, 246. On the Stoic aspects of Percy's writings, see Lewis A. Lawson, "Walker Percy's Southern Stoic," *Southern Literary Journal* 3 (Fall 1976): 5–31, and Lawson, "*The Moviegoer* and the Stoic Heritage," in Duane J. MacMillan, ed., *The Stoic Strain in American Literature* (Toronto, 1979), 179–91.

27. Percy, *Lancelot*, 157, 158, 159, 213.

28. See Carroll B. Johnson, *Madness and Lust: A Psychoanalytical Approach to Don Quixote* (Berkeley, 1983), 68–76 passim; Pedro Calderón de la Barca, *Secret Vengeance for Secret Insult*, in *Four Plays*, trans. Edwin Honig (New York, 1961), act 3, pp. 53, 54. See also Edwin Honig, *Calderón and the Seizures of Honor* (Cambridge, Mass., 1972), 37–52; Percy, *Lancelot*, 154–55, 242.

29. Brinkmeyer, *Three Catholic Writers*, 157; Corinne Dale, "*Lancelot* and the Medieval Quests of Sir Lancelot and Dante," in Jac Tharpe, ed., *Walker Percy: Art and Ethics* (Jackson, Miss., 1980), 99–100; Percy, *Lancelot*, 21, 155. See also Lewis A. Lawson, "William Alexander Percy, Walker Percy, and the Apocalypse," in Lawson, *Another Generation: Southern Fiction Since World War II* (Jackson, Miss., 1984), 122–43.

30. Calderón, *Secret Vengeance for Secret Insult*, act 3, p. 71. It is interesting that images of wind and storm in Calderón and the hurricane backdrop in *Lancelot* both symbolize the way in which the characters are driven by forces of anarchy, as if a mindless god rules. See Honig, *Calderón*, 24–27.

31. Percy, *Lancelot*, 138.

32. John Kennedy Toole, *A Confederacy of Dunces* (Baton Rouge, 1980), 30.

33. Ibid., 191–92, 281.

34. Harry Crews, *Karate Is a Thing of the Spirit* (New York, 1983 [1972]).

35. The midget Munroe appears as a full character and in a different role in *This Thing Don't Lead to Heaven* (New York, 1970). See Crews, *Karate*, 42.

36. Frank W. Shelton, "Harry Crews: Man's Search for Perfection," *Southern*

Literary Journal 12 (Spring 1980): 97–113. Like Percy, Crews denies association with a southern school of writing or tradition. See ibid., 97–98.

37. Harry Crews, *The Gospel Singer* (New York, 1968); Flannery O'Connor, *Wise Blood*, in *Three* (New York, 1960); Walker Percy, *Love in the Ruins: The Adventures of a Bad Catholic at a Time Near the End of the World* (New York, 1978 [1971]); Barry Hannah, *Ray* (New York, 1981), 54. Also see John Griffin Jones, ed., *Mississippi Writers Talking* (Jackson, Miss., 1982), 138, 143, 147–48.

38. Fred Hobson, ed., *South-Watching: Selected Essays by Gerald W. Johnson* (Chapel Hill, 1983), 88. William Styron argues, "Younger writers like Barry Hannah and Bobbie Ann Mason do capture a flavor of the South, but I don't know if it makes much difference any longer, whether the voice is so distinctive as to make it peculiarly Southern anymore." James L. W. West III, ed., *Conversations with William Styron* (Jackson, Miss., 1985), 267.

39. Padgett Powell, *Edisto* (New York, 1983), 9–10.

40. Simpson, *The Dispossessed Garden*, 86.

The South
in Southern Agrarianism

Paul K. Conkin

M y topic may seem familiar, yet in many ways it remains an almost lost souvenir of the depression thirties. Most people know about an elusive, provocative, confusing book called *I'll Take My Stand*. It has, in effect, camouflaged rather than illuminated the story of southern agrarianism. Yet the book did launch a movement through its introductory statement of principles, a delightful parody of Marx and Engels' *Communist Manifesto*. This statement contained a critique of collectivized, centralized production of goods and services in large firms, those with a narrow managerial elite and insecure and servile employees. Confusingly, the group of Vanderbilt professors who with others put together this book called their enemy "industrialism." What the diverse authors did not clarify, perhaps could not then clarify except negatively, was the implied opposite—a humane and nonexploitative economic system, one which they simply identified as agrarian.[1]

The twelve writers could not fill in the positive content because they never agreed on what a good society was or the means of achieving it. Images of an organic, feudal, established, hierarchical society always warred with images of a society made up of independent yeomen. Three of the contributors—Bruce Kline, Stark Young, and Herman C. Nixon—were barely able to endorse the manifesto and never supported the subsequent agrarian movement. Another contributor, John Gould Fletcher, the mentally beset expatriate Arkansas poet, continued to identify with the agrarians, but embarrassed all the others by his extremism. In the early thirties he literally wanted to restore the Ancien Régime, to move back to a formal aristocracy and an established church. This leaves only eight authors who, despite profound differences, joined together in a reasonably co-

131

herent crusade, one that remained vital and influential from 1930 to 1938.

Four were most deeply involved and provided the leadership for a loosely organized movement that attracted converts all over the South. The ablest, the most philosophical, but one of the more flexible advocats was John Crowe Ransom, the earlier Fugitive poet, a brilliant literary critic, and until 1937 a professor of English at Vanderbilt. Briefly, Ransom became a dedicated political activist, and used critical essays on Milton to demonstrate that a prophetic involvement in political and economic issues did not violate one's first calling as an artist. Less philosophical, more dogmatic, more emotionally involved, but much better informed on southern history and on economic issues, was Frank Owsley, for the whole eight years a history professor at Vanderbilt. Younger, more radical in bent, was Allen Tate, a former Vanderbilt student, a Fugitive poet, a pungent literary critic, who in 1930, after a brief career as a free-lance writer in New York and then in Paris, moved to a farm near Clarksville, Tennessee, close to his friends in Nashville. Finally, Donald Davidson, of the Vanderbilt English Department, a gifted lyrical poet, an eloquent essayist, belligerently independent but at times naive on economic issues, deeply, even passionately loyal to his native Upper South, gave his all to the movement but was often idiosyncratic in his interpretation of the new gospel.

Less critically involved were four other men, all with some connection to Vanderbilt and Nashville. The most committed of these was Andrew Lytle, a former Vanderbilt student, a dramatist and novelist, even at times an actor in an alien New York City, deeply loyal to his native Tennessee, so angry at Yankee civilization and big business as to sound, at times, like the shrillest Communist party writer of the thirties. Much more detached, and the most empirical and scholarly in his approach to southern problems, was Lyle Lanier, until 1937 an academically frustrated assistant professor of psychology at Vanderbilt, a faculty ally of Ransom and Owsley in extended skirmishes with the central administration of Vanderbilt. Less involved in the hard economic issues, but one who lived as well as celebrated the benefits of farm life, was John Donald Wade, who taught in the Vanderbilt English Department from 1930 to 1934, only then to retreat back to his Georgia farm and to part-time teaching at the University of Georgia. Least involved personally was Robert Penn Warren, then a young but budding poet and novelist, a former student of Ransom and Davidson, who taught for three years on an interim basis in the Vanderbilt English Department before finding a full-time job at Louisiana State University in 1934.

I'll Take My Stand triggered more southern discussion and criticism than the authors expected. Ransom and Davidson, in particular, defended the book in well-publicized debates, debates soon colored by the developing depression. The book proved infinitely confusing, for it spoke with several voices. This helped ensure its continued vitality, for one or another emphasis has remained persuasive for audiences all the way to the present. It was this opening manifesto, plus certain themes in key essays by Ransom, Tate, and Davidson, that gained the favorable attention of anti-modernist critics outside the South. Events, most of all the depression, plus the challenge of nonsouthern sympathizers, all helped push these eight southerners toward a reasonably coherent economic ideology and program by 1933, one that complemented but did not duplicate the concerns that led to *I'll Take My Stand*. For example, the original idea for a symposium on the South sprang from the Scopes trial at Dayton, Tennessee, and the perceived need by young men in the South for a sophisticated defense of their section and, in a sense, their own identity as southerners. In the prosperous twenties, the business decade, they were not yet as aware, as they would soon become in the developing depression, of the economic problems that haunted the South and in particular southern agriculture.

The 1930 manifesto remains a powerful statement, loaded in language, deliberately polemical in form. It was a call to arms to southerners threatened by "industrialism," a label that most agrarians changed after 1930 to "corporate capitalism" or just "capitalism." Briefly, industrialism referred to all collectivized forms of production, even that in agriculture. An industrial economy is made up of large accumulations of capital, directed by a few managers, and dependent upon the labor of nonpropertied, thus dependent and thus servile, wage laborers. The manifesto remained distinctive in agrarian literature because of the philosophical nuances contributed by its principal author, Ransom. Central to his argument, one shared with Marxists, was the primacy of productive arrangements in determining all facets of a culture. Thus, an agrarian economy fostered a respect for nature, a flowering of the arts of good living, and an openness to religious myth, all either precluded or distorted by industrialism. In an industrial society the main victims are the alienated workers, those who groan under the system, who have no intrinsic involvement with the ends of work, who suffer from insecurity and a hurried, even frantic industrial regimen, who know only the brutalizing effects and none of the joys of work, and who gain only the satisfaction of an almost mindless consumption. Note that these issues—the problem of alienated workers, the hazards of unchecked economic growth, the lost respect for nature, and a lamented decline in the arts or in religion—have permeated most modern social criticism, either from the left or the right.[2]

The manifesto was most distinctive in its wholehearted rejection of any further collectivism as a cure for modern problems. The socialist goal of worker ownership was delusive, for it threatened not only less economic efficiency (not a major concern of agrarians) but even less freedom and dignity and artistry for workers. Yet, to the agrarians, a communist society was a logical outcome of industrialism, a further extension of existing forms of corporate collectivism. Almost perversely, but suggestively, the agrarians often made capitalism and communism synonymous terms. Tate would later argue that capitalism and socialism were both names for an attack upon property. Owsley, in a bitter reaction to the Scottsboro trials, distinguished two types of industrialists—the capitalist and the proletarian. At the same time, the agrarians argued that ameliorative reforms could not repair the fundamental evils of industrialism. The countervailing power of unions, state regulation, and welfare transfers were all only ways of rearranging the economic foliage, said Tate. They never touched the root of the problem, which required a revolutionary answer. And, in Tate's view, only reaction could be truly revolutionary.[3]

The Great Depression made the early agrarians prophets in ways they never expected in 1930. The industrial machine, which they had castigated for its dehumanizing effects, now seemed tarnished by its economic failures. The agrarians had applauded, above all else, a nonacquisitive economy, one that allowed *leisure,* the most pregnant word in *I'll Take My Stand. Leisure* meant, not idleness, but artful work pursued for humane ends at a leisurely pace without the discipline of bosses or time clocks. In the prosperous twenties the agrarians had identified the primary evil of modernity as employment. Suddenly the great perceived malady was unemployment. To them, it was simply the other side of the coin—an inevitable, always potential consequence of employment and its insecurities. Now, in the depression, they believed they might be able to offer an appealing solution to American ills, a solution that would lead unemployed Americans, and soon some employed ones as well, out of an industrial economy. Despite all of its problems, the South might lead the way towards such a solution. But prior to launching their crusade for a new and yet an old answer, they had, in a sense, to discover property. After 1933, *property* replaced *leisure* as the key word in the agrarian vocabulary.

In 1930 Tate, Ransom, and Davidson sparred with Paul Elmer More and Irving Babbitt, the Harvard gurus of a classically rooted "New Humanism." Although Tate and Ransom knew the work of two comparable

English writers, Hilaire Belloc and G. K. Chesterton, they did not at first acknowledge the influence of distributism, the small English movement (a league, two periodicals, dozens of propagandists) founded by Belloc. This changed after 1933. The New Humanists, distributists, and southern agrarians publicly affirmed their common cause in the midst of a world-wide depression. In 1933 journalist Seward Collins began publication of the new *American Review,* a journal promoted as a forum for all anti-modernist movements. Unfortunately for the later reputation of the journal, Collins revealed his personal infatuation with Italian fascism. In the pages of the *Review,* the southern agrarians fully adopted the ideology of the distributists and used this perspective to address southern issues. Their developed position finally qualified them as true agrarians, not just sentimental celebrants of farm life, which had become the distorted meaning of the word *agrarian* in twentieth-century America. They now embraced the radical implications of land reform, of taking property from monopolistic owners and opening up access to nature for everyone. Tate, the most radical, wanted to confiscate the property of what he called the "money power."

The southern agrarians now realized that what industrialism had meant all along was the gradual destruction of property, along with manageable, personalized, household forms of production. The modern corporation had slowly destroyed property and free enterprise, even as it reduced the majority of humankind to wage dependency and a type of slavery. In England, Belloc had launched a crusade for the restoration of a rooted and stable English peasantry as an antidote to an otherwise inevitable socialist or fascist form of totalitarianism. He had advocated a series of state initiatives, including carefully targeted taxes, to foster and protect not only family-owned farms but small manufacturers and retail shops. Such a crucial state role was necessary because open competition ensured the eventual ascendancy of larger and larger firms, as Marxists argued. Obviously, by property, Belloc meant not consumer goods or investment paper but the means of production—land and tools. Only a secure access to these allowed people to escape servile dependency, to gain independence and freedom, even the freedom requisite to responsible citizenship. If this reminds you of eighteenth-century libertarian thought, so be it.[4]

The southern agrarians welcomed such reminders of Thomas Jefferson. They proclaimed property restoration as a return to a traditional American ideal. Tate, in particular, loved this analysis. In an essay published in the *American Review* he tried to disabuse Americans of their corrupted uses of the word *property.* Much influenced, as was Ransom, by Adolf A.

Berle, Jr., and Gardiner C. Means's landmark 1932 book *The Modern Corporation and Private Property*, he demonstrated the widespread and increasing separation of paper claims on profits from managerial responsiblity. For Tate, any ownership apart from management, from a personal and moral responsibility for the use of capital, did not qualify as property. By the same perspective, Ransom referred to modern investors as economic geldings, emasculated and irresponsible owners with no effective control over what happened to their so-called property. And corporate managers, like overseers on antebellum southern plantations, did not own land and capital and had no personal responsibility for its humane use and no paternal regard for workers. As powerful but irresponsible hirelings, they served only two urgent goals—maximizing the profits of owners and protecting or increasing their own salaries and power.[5]

This understanding of a corporate or collective economy clarified the reform goals of the agrarians. They wanted to preserve the remnants of a proprietary society, a society everywhere threatened but still dominant in agriculture. But farmers, particularly those in the South, suffered from deep maladies, some rooted in national policy, some in their own capitulation to the values of an industrial order. Thus, at one level, the agrarians tried to find solutions to the economic disabilities of farmers in the thirties. Beyond this, they tried to motivate farmers to turn, in part, away from commercial, commodity production, away from their vulnerability to competitive prices, and back far enough toward self-providence as to bring market production in line with demand. In addition, they offered a widely applauded solution in 1933–34 to massive unemployment. As so many others, including President Roosevelt, they believed the late twenties had marked the apex of economic growth. Our very productive manufacturers could never reabsorb most laid-off workers. These people needed, not an endless dole, but help to purchase subsistence plots so they might live with only part-time employment. The southern agrarians greeted a small subsistence homesteads program in the New Deal, but soon despaired of its limited scope and nonagrarian values. Finally, for the economy as a whole, the agrarians joined in antimonopoly crusades, in attacks on concentrated wealth, in support of vigorous antitrust enforcement, local handicrafts and folk arts, and openly discriminatory taxes against great wealth, or in any measures that would help decentralize production and bring it back as close as possible to the household or proprietary ideal, even if such meant some loss in efficiency.[6]

This completes a too-hurried summary of the generalized position advanced by the agrarians. To what South did they direct their critique? Despite telling differences on critical issues, they shared some common historical and cultural perspectives. One confusion was that of the South's boundaries. They did not ignore this issue. They frequently acknowledged both tremendous cultural diversity in the South and the many blurred boundaries that never allowed any sharp distinctions. At times, southernness became their subject, not a geographical section as much as beliefs and values that might be found in the Midwest or even in rural New England. But most often they leaned back on history: the South consisted of the eleven Confederate states, with Kentucky and Maryland at times pulled in because of cultural commonalities. The former Unionist areas of Appalachia received favorable notices, not much more. Because of an admittedly trans-Appalachian bias, the Chesapeake and Tidewater South remained distant, while the heavily industrialized Piedmont scarcely figured at all in their analysis.

From a contemporary perspective, the historically most distinctive characteristic of their delimited South had to be its biracial makeup. Despite Texas Hispanics, Louisiana Cajuns, and widespread clusters of Germans, this South was settled, its culture largely shaped, by several tribes from both Britain and Africa. The Negro, in a sense, was omnipresent in agrarian images of the South. So was a Negro problem, which so divided the individual agrarians that they could never agree on any but generalized economic solutions for blacks. But, from a present perspective, what is surprising is how much even those, such as Lanier, Ransom, and Warren, who would soon embrace black equality, still viewed blacks as an unwanted burden, as cultural appendages or parasites. They revealed little appreciation of how much British and African cultures mixed and merged in the South, of how much blacks influenced southern religion, cuisine, music, and literature. Others, such as Davidson, Owsley, and Lytle, not only slighted the black influence but put blacks down by nasty, racist statements.

Perhaps appropriately, their broadest, most determining commonality was a view of southern history. Owsley served as a blunt, at times tactless, spokesman, but every agrarian seemed to accept his overall version of the southern past. After all, few voices of historical dissent, even in the North, disturbed their outlook in the thirties. Reinforcement came from Charles A. Beard, from the Dunning School, even from Marxists. Davidson claimed the whole Mississippi Valley Historical Association as a buttress to the agrarian view, for its leading historians had all rebelled against the monopolistic Northeast.

In Owsley's sharp language, all American history, from the capitalist corrupted Constitutional Convention in 1787 to the subsequent conflict between Hamilton and Jefferson all the way to the 1930s, had been one unrelenting battle between industrialists and agrarians. The irrepressible Civil War marked only a climactic episode in the ongoing struggle. In the early nineteenth century, the industrialists' cause remained a powerful but clearly a minority cause, even in the North. Thus, Andrew Lytle wrote a long celebration of John Taylor and his early indictment of a developing aristocracy of paper and patronage, of a soon-to-be capitalist class, first of merchants and financiers, then of factory owners, that would reduce most of the former yeomen of the West into wage slavery. The vulnerable majority of artisans and farmers tried to defend their proprietary, nonacquisitive values, against overwhelming odds. Jefferson and Andrew Jackson symbolized resistance, yet in each case compromised the cause. Only the South, with a largely agricultural economy, remained firm in its resistance to industrialism. And even it had defectors, while the rare, large absentee-owned plantations, cursed by the overseer system, had prefigured modern industrialism. But for the most part southern production took place in households, however extended, and under the paternal direction of owners. Property induced responsibility, good citizenship. Slavery, however atrocious in theory, was, in Ransom's term, mild in effect, for black servants functioned as dependents in a highly personalized, organic context. Most master-servant relationships remained personal, caring, even as work was leisurely and relaxed.[7]

The South, in defense of such an agrarian order, eventually seceded, fought a war for its independence and lost. Northern industrialists, who had heretofore hidden their predatory goals behind the moral abstractions of abolitionists, now had a free hand in shaping policies conducive to corporate collectivisim. Even the illegitimately ratified Fourteenth Amendment, ostensibly a protection of Negro rights, became a legal tool for solidifying a new industrial regimen and a new monied aristocracy aligned with the Republican party.

The South could only suffer the consequences of defeat. First came the agonies of black rule and Radical Reconstruction. In none of the agrarians do I find the slightest reservation about the then still dominant view of Reconstruction. They did not like the sentimentality of *Gone With the Wind;* they shared Margaret Mitchell's historical outlook. After redemption, the South suffered a continued colonial status. Northern economic policies—monetary restraint, high tariffs, corporate subsidies, tax policy, unequal rail rates—all discriminated against the South, against farmers, and against most small-scale producers. Images of the war prevented the natural alliance of South and Midwest. And, slowly, even conscientious southerners, desperate to break from the bonds of poverty, began to flirt with the industrial ideal, to sell out their own heritage. However mistaken, the New South movement was at least understandable, for the South paid a dear price for its undying dream of proprietorship and freedom. Yet the dream lived on, more compelling in the South than in any other section. And, despite all the maladies, despite incomes less than 50 percent of the national average, much of the supportive economic order remained. In 1930 approximately 60 percent of southerners lived in villages and rural areas, approximately 40 percent worked in agriculture, with perhaps another 20 percent in services or first-level processing directly tied to agriculture.

By 1930 the long struggle seemed almost over. Even southerners had increasingly despaired of the fight or had already deserted the cause. Thus, the role of the southern agrarians was to rally the discouraged troops, to try and set up some final defense and, with the enemy temporarily discredited by the awful depression, launch a small counteroffensive. Of course, they lost this final battle. They sensed they would lose even in 1933 or 1934. But, armed at least with eloquence, they lent an element of nobility to the final denouement.

The agrarians believed that a culture rested upon economic foundations. In the absence of a proprietary foundation, the cultural icons of an agrarian society were bound to degenerate into the romantic sentiments that pervaded *Gone With the Wind,* or into the gothic romances that industrialized, urban southerners still escape to in their rare moments away from frenzied consumption or the opiate of television screens. What were these icons? Briefly, the more literary agrarians tried to flesh out the meaning of civility and gentility. They believed that rural southerners had kept their strong ties to place, to the land, and still yearned for the independence made possible only by property. They rejected unrelievably acquisitive values, worked at a leisurely pace, cultivated the arts of good living, loved storytelling, and, perhaps most critical, knew and accepted their dependence upon an often unpredictable natural order. Such southerners may not have been sensitive to natural beauty; rural people often took this for granted. But they knew awe, fear, insecurity. This, said the agrarians, led to mythic, nonscientific, and nondirective ways of conceptualizing nature and experience. Such a mythic response underwrote religious piety and created the necessary conditions for a great literature. Southerners were more religious and more poetic than Yankees. Tate and Ransom, with great subtlety, explored the issue of religion in the South. They defended the religious impulse of southerners but were often distressed at the doctrines and practice of evangelical Protestants. Lytle, Davidson, and Owsley, without a hint of subtlety or theological sophistication, almost belligerently defended the existing conservative or funda-

139

mentalist forms of southern Christianity against secular or liberal alternatives. Later they would view southern agrarianism largely as a defense of religious values, or conversely as a defense against atheistic communism. Of course, the agrarians also acknowledged some of the darker aspects of southern culture, such as a horrible propensity to violence, but tried to explain most vices and excesses as inevitable products of economic exploitation, of poverty, or outside agitation of the race issue.

Both their version of southern history and their characterization of a distinctive southern culture beg a whole range of empirical issues. I am not qualified to arbitrate any of those. This is not the time. I doubt if anyone knows enough to offer conclusive answers. Certainly, half-truths inform both their historical and cultural myths. In a sense, what is remarkable about the early thirties is how little anyone knew about the South. In the absence of knowledge, impressions had to guide. I am still inclined to smile indulgently when anyone offers his version of a distinctive southern mind or culture. I remain skeptical of even the most nuanced and brilliant versions, from a W. J. Cash to a Bertram Wyatt-Brown.

In 1930 it was easy for Ransom or Lytle to romanticize an ideal. By 1933 it was difficult to fit such an ideal to the reality of southern agriculture in a period of crisis. The more Ransom learned about the realities of southern life, its diversity, complexities, and overwhelming problems, the less he felt free to talk about it at all. In the face of a rural South blighted by economic inefficiency, underemployed workers, undercapitalized farms, backward or ignorant farming practices, insecure ownership, tenancy rates approaching 50 percent, terrible public services, ill-funded schools, meager public health facilities, monotonous and unhealthy diets, widespread violence, and racial fears and resentments, how could anyone oppose new manufacturing and service industries? The agrarians accepted this dilemma. To win their battle, they had to find ways of solving the South's agricultural problems. They needed specific proposals, not a philosophical defense of property and freedom. Thus, in March of 1935 Owsley published an essay entitled "The Pillars of Agrarianism." This was, by intent, the programmatic sequel to *I'll Take My Stand*. Owsley cleared it with other agrarians, and from then on most of them deferred to it when pressed for practical answers to southern problems. Owsley distributed the essay widely among politicians. It may have had limited impact on the Bankhead-Jones Farm Tenancy Act of 1936.

In his first pillar, Owsley offered political schemes to rehabilitate southern agriculture, using as a model the Scandinavian countries. To a large extent he embraced New Deal agricultural programs, including easier credit and price supports. He urged a tenant purchase plan, and wanted federal and state governments to buy up all bank and absentee-owned or excessive acreage owned by planters and use this for a new homestead program for those with farming skills (eighty acres, a log house, two mules and two cows, and living expenses for the first year). Consistent with traditional agrarian principles, these homesteads were to be unalienable, neither saleable nor mortgageable. He also endorsed laws that would prevent land speculation. For the urban employee without agricultural skills, or for low skilled blacks, he proposed apprenticeship programs on larger plantations. In three other pillars, he advocated special soil conservation and rehabilitation programs, with stringent penalties for private abuses of the land; subsistence farming to control market surpluses; and special subsidies to farmers to balance the tariff protection or monopolistic market control enjoyed by the manufacturing and commercial sectors. Finally, in the least plausible pillar, but by now the major commitment of Donald Davidson, he proposed a constitutional amendment that would divide the United States into economically rational regions, each with its own government and each with protective vetoes over threatening federal policies, a scheme which reminds one of the strategies of John C. Calhoun.[8]

In a sense, the southern agrarians made their last stand in 1936. Tate joined with Herbert Agar, the Louisville historian and journalist, by then a close friend and an advocate of decentralization and property redistribution, to publish a second symposium, *Who Owns America?* The distributists and humanists joined, and set the agenda for the volume. All eight agrarians contributed, but Lanier's scholarly analysis of business concentration, his proposals for increased regulation and in rare cases public ownership, only indirectly supported the agrarian cause. Warren wrote a delightful but not very self-revealing contrast of proletarian and regional writers. Davidson offered an eloquent plea for regional autonomy. Owsley rehearsed again his indictment of the devil Hamilton and all his legacies. Tate most clearly and forcefully supported a redistribution of property. Ransom, in one of his last detours from literary criticism into the treacherous area of public advocacy, wrote eloquently about the problems of farmers, and advocated relief in rather orthodox New Deal terms (subsidies, better schools, and cheap TVA-like electricity). Such aid might enable more farmers to remain on the land. But in any case, many southerners would remain employees, for some production required the efficiency of factories. For such employees he also recommended standard New Deal remedies—bargaining power for unions, unemployment insurance, improved housing, medical care, good schools, and, most intriguing, workplace rules that would accommodate the naturally slower tempo of southern life, work rules that he also advocated for the North. Even Tate grudgingly admitted the necessities of some factories, but he argued that workers should be able to dictate what they produced. Visible in these essays, which for over half the eight would be their last published stand in behalf of agrarianism, were divergent emphases that would soon destroy any semblance of unity, any common purposes to give focus to a movement.[9]

In 1937–38 the southern agrarians slipped into silence. The *American Review* stopped publication in 1938. The last two volumes contained a few reviews, but nothing new or original, from the agrarians. In 1937 Ransom left Vanderbilt for Kenyon College; in 1938 Lanier moved to Vassar. Both gave up on agrarianism. Warren had long since identified with the movement more out of friendship with his mentors than out of conviction. For Wade, a spirited defense of rural life or a castigation of the arrogant and manipulative views of nature fostered by a parasitic urban culture had been more important than any political program. Tate shifted his interest almost entirely back to literature and to religion as he moved toward a 1950 conversion to Catholicism. Until their death both Davidson and Owsley maintained the faith, at least as they understood it. Lytle still supports the cause. But who cared?

The golden moment had passed. The depression interlude proved an exception, a detour in American history, not the opening of a new era of retrenchment and stability. The intellectual openness of the early thirties, the luxuriant sprouting of all manner of strange ideological plants, gave way to the orthodoxy of a regulatory-welfare state. In Tate's language, we only rearranged some foliage, made cosmetic changes. To his despair, the American public came to accept, if not love, the new look. They certainly did not want to dig at any of the roots. American farmers, instead of seeking a secure refuge from the insecurities of an international market, soon began their desperate love affair with efficiency, effecting after World War II the clearest industrial revolution in all of our history. Instead of accommodating new people, going back to subsistence, a highly capitalized agriculture in only fifty years would eliminate approximately 90 percent of the family farms that existed in 1930.

The South accommodated the agricultural revolution more slowly than the North, and suffered some of the consequences in lower incomes. But today, except in some favored areas such as the Mississippi Delta, agriculture has become a minor southern industry, close to being a hobby or a tax dodge for people employed in nonagricultural industries. In few areas of the South can one find even one family whose total income derives from farming. Instead, the South is the new manufacturing capital of the country. Despite a closing gap in incomes, despite the Sun Belt phenomena, despite the miracle of air conditioning, the industrial foliage has not changed that much. Wages remain below national averages, fewer workers enjoy the protection of union representation and bargaining, state regulations tend to be more lax than those in the North, state-shared welfare transfers are well below national averages, and a whole array of public services remain ill-funded in comparison to those in the North. Thus, not only has industrialism conquered the South but in its worst possible dress.

The main bent of the agrarians was openly, even boastfully, reactionary. They wanted to reverse existing trends, repudiate progress, go back to earlier ideals, restore values now all but lost. And whatever the oversimplifications in their descriptions of American society, the mythical content of their historical and cultural judgments, they were correct in one sense. An earlier America, whatever the compensatory costs, had realized, as perhaps no other society in modern history, the proprietary ideal. Nowhere else had small owners enjoyed, or suffered, as much control over land and tools as did American farmers and artisans in the early nineteenth century. For Belloc, the unlimited freedom had been part of the problem. Open competition, joined with acquisitive values, ensured the growth of what the agrarians called industrialism. One could not have it both ways. He believed an enduring, propertied society required various safeguards and restrictions on owners, something close to a feudal or a peasant-type society, one with inhibited mobility, sanctions against large plots, and laws to keep land off the market. Tate and Ransom thought they glimpsed such an established or traditional European-like society in the Old South. Their organic images clashed with the more libertarian and populistic values of a Lytle or an Owsley. Lytle idealized the vulgar, bumptious, independent backwoods types found in the most provincial areas of the South. But even in Owsley the organic motif lingered in his proposals to take land off the market, to forbid speculation, to use an apprenticeship system for less able or less skilled homesteaders.

The closest comparison to the program of the distributist-agrarians has been that of latter-day single-tax advocates. Both agrarians and single taxers proposed economically radical but noncollectivist answers to the perceived injustices of a speculative and profit-oriented economy. Henry George sought ways of taking land off the market, of eliminating unfair speculative gains and thus opening up nature for those who would use it. In a sense, he represented the culmination of nineteenth-century agrarianism, a loose movement that stretched back to the most radical workingmen's associations of the 1830s. In Scandinavia, single-tax parties survive to the present. And, almost unnoticed, in the late sixties and early seventies a few scattered groups joined in efforts to expand ownership, with John McClaughry, a special assistant to President Nixon, as the most visible spokesman. But, as one might suspect, the latter-day advocates of wider ownership have often included home ownership, even corporate stock, as authentic examples of property. They have also joined with movements in behalf of more social responsibility on the part of large corporations. One can hear the agrarians groaning in their graves. For whatever else they were, they were radicals, not accommodationists. They tried to get at the roots of modern ills, and wanted drastic, structural changes in our modern corporate economy.

They accepted the high risks. They knew it was not easy to restore property even to a majority of American families. Drastically lower living standards was only the first of many possible costs. The perceived rewards, as so eloquently advertised by the agrarians, may have briefly seemed worth the sacrifice in the midst of a depression. Not for long. Independence, leisure, piety, and a taste for poetry are, as I gauge contemporary values, well down the list, trivial beside career success, expressive freedoms, and a heady dose of consumptive pleasures, all gained by a productive system legally stripped of the worst abuses and indignities of the past. As a despairing Owsley put it, without a realistic chance of regaining property, most Americans will continue to vote for policies that maintain them as well-fed hirelings. As one of those who so votes, I cannot help but feel a twinge of guilt. I am not sure I like myself for going along with the existing system. To the accusing agrarians, I have sold my soul to the devil for a good mess of porridge.

Notes

1. Twelve Southerners, *I'll Take My Stand: The South and the Agrarian Tradition* (New York, 1962), xix–xxx.

2. Ibid.

3. Allen Tate, "Spengler's Tract Against Liberalism," *American Review* 3 (April 1934): 41–47; Frank Owsley, "Scottsboro, the Sequel to Abolition and Reconstruction," *American Review* 1 (June 1933): 257–85.

4. See Hilaire Belloc, "The Restoration of Property," *American Review* 1 (April, May, June, September, October 1933): 1–16, 204–19, 344–57, 468–82, 600–69; 2 (November 1933): 46–57.

5. Allen Tate, "Notes on Liberty and Property, *American Review* 6 (March 1936): 596–611; John Crowe Ransom, "What Does the South Want?" in *Who*

Owns America? ed. Herbert Agar and Allen Tate (Boston, 1936), 178–93; Jess Gilbert and Steve Brown, "Alternative Land Reform Proposals in the 1930s: The Nashville Agrarians and the Southern Tenant Farmers' Union," *Agricultural History* 55 (October 1981): 352–58.

6. Paul K. Conkin, *Tomorrow a New World: The New Deal Community Program* (Ithaca, 1959), 93–130.

7. Donald Davidson, "Lands That Were Golden," *American Review* 3 (October 1934): 546–61, and 3 (November 1934): 29–55; Andrew Lytle, "John Taylor and the Political Economy of Agrarianism," *American Review* 3 (September and October 1934): 432–47, 630–43, and 4 (November 1934): 84–99; Frank Owsley, "The Old South and the New," *American Review* 6 (February 1936): 475–85.

8. Frank Owsley, "The Pillars of Agrarianism," *American Review* 4 (March 1935): 529–47.

9. See the essays by Lyle Lanier, Frank Owsley, Allen Tate, Donald Davidson, John Crowe Ransom, Andrew Lytle, John Donald Wade, and Robert Penn Warren in *Who Owns America?*

Contributors

PAUL K. CONKIN is Distinguished Professor of History, Vanderbilt University. His numerous books and articles include *Puritans and Pragmatists; Self-Evident Truths; Prophets of Prosperity; Gone With the Ivy: A Biography of Vanderbilt University;* and *Big Daddy From the Pedernales,* a biography of Lyndon B. Johnson.

ERIC FONER is Professor of History at Columbia University. His works include *Free Soil, Free Labor, Free Men; Tom Paine and Revolutionary America; Politics and Ideology in the Age of the Civil War;* and *Nothing But Freedom: Emancipation and Its Legacy.*

ELIZABETH FOX-GENOVESE is Director of Women's Studies, Emory University. She is author of *The Origins of Physiocracy* and coauthor of *Fruits of Merchant Capital.*

GEORGE M. FREDRICKSON is Edgar E. Robinson Professor of History at Stanford University. Among his books are *The Black Image in the White Mind; A Nation Divided;* and *White Supremacy: A Comparative Study in American and South African History.*

EUGENE D. GENOVESE is Professor of History, University of Rochester. Professor Genovese is the author of *The Political Economy of Slavery; The World the Slaveholders Made; Roll, Jordan, Roll;* and (with Elizabeth Fox-Genovese) *Fruits of Merchant Capital.*

NELL IRVIN PAINTER is Professor of History, University of North Carolina at Chapel Hill. She is the author of *Exodusters; The Narrative of Hosea Hudson;* and *Disquieting Portents: The United States, 1886–1919.*

IMMANUEL WALLERSTEIN is Professor of Sociology at the State University of New York at Binghamton. His works include *The Modern World-*

147

System; The Capitalist World-Economy; and *The Politics of the World-Economy.*

JOEL WILLIAMSON is Lineberger Professor in the Humanities, University of North Carolina at Chapel Hill. He is the author of *After Slavery: The Negro in South Carolina; New People: Miscegenation and Mulattoes in the United States;* and *The Crucible of Race.*

BERTRAM WYATT-BROWN is Milbauer Professor of History at the University of Florida. Among his works are *Lewis Tappan and the Evangelical War Against Slavery; The American People in the Antebellum South; Southern Honor;* and *Yankee Saints and Southern Sinners.*